Not Settling

For Less

Things Aren't What They Seem

DONELL JACKSON

SHIFT ELEMENTS LLC
5830 E 2ND ST, STE 7000 #9190
CASPER, WY 82607
SEND FEEDBACK TO INFO@SHIFTELEMENTS.COM
COPYRIGHT © 2024 BY DONELL JACKSON.

ISBN: SOFTCOVER: 9798330448548
EBOOK: 9798330448371

SPECIAL DISCOUNTS FOR BULK FOR BOOKSTORE PLACEMENT IS AVAILABLE. PLEASE CONTACT INFO@SHIFTELEMENTS.COM

A Couple Reasons Why You Should Settle

<u>A C</u>OUPLE OF <u>R</u>EASONS WHY YOU <u>S</u>HOULDN'T SETTLE

<u>S</u>ETTLING <u>O</u>NLY <u>B</u>RINGS <u>R</u>ESENTMENT

YOU MAY NOT SEE IT AS AN ISSUE, BUT IF YOU SETTLE FOR SOMEONE, CHANCES ARE THEY WILL NEVER LIVE UP TO YOUR EXPECTATIONS. IF YOU KEEP EXPECTING HIM/HER TO BE SOMETHING THEY ARE NOT, YOU'LL ONLY BECOME UNHAPPY AND DISAPPOINTED, AND THEY WILL ALWAYS FAIL BECAUSE YOU CAN'T CHANGE SOMEONE. SO, DON'T TRY.

<u>Y</u>OU'RE <u>G</u>OING <u>T</u>O <u>H</u>AVE <u>A</u>N <u>U</u>NSTABLE <u>R</u>ELATIONSHIP

WHEN YOU SETTLE, YOUR RELATIONSHIP IS GOING TO BECOME UNDESIRABLE. BOTH PARTIES MUST WANT TO IMPRESS AND BRING A BIT OF ROMANCE INTO THE RELATIONSHIP (CANDLE-LITE DINNERS, ROMANTIC GESTURES, COMPLIMENTS, ETC.). IF YOU FEEL LIKE YOU'VE SETTLED, WHY TAKE YOURSELF THROUGH THE TROUBLE TO IMPRESS THE OTHER PERSON? YOU'RE ALWAYS GOING TO FEEL LIKE THAT PERSON OWES YOU

Not Settling for Less

SOMETHING, SO THE CHANCES OF YOU BEING SPONTANEOUS AND GENERATING A SPARK ARE SLIM TO NONE.

YOU WON'T BE SEXUALLY SATISFIED

EVERYONE HAS WITNESSED SOMEONE WHO CAN'T PERFORM TO THEIR STANDARDS IN THE BEDROOM. JUST KNOW THAT IF YOU SETTLE, YOU ARE CREATING THE POSSIBILITY THAT YOU WILL NEVER BE FULLY SATISFIED. IT WILL MOST LIKELY BE A MEANS TO AN END (WHATEVER YOUR REASON IS FOR SETTLING). JUST MAKE SURE YOU'RE HAPPY AND ALWAYS REMEMBER: SEX SHOULD NEVER FEEL LIKE AN OBLIGATION.

A Couple Reasons Why You Should Settle

DON'T GET MARRIED JUST BECAUSE "IT SOUNDS NICE"

DON'T SETTLE JUST BECAUSE YOU DON'T WANT TO BE THE "LAST ONE STANDING" WHILE ALL YOUR FRIENDS ARE GETTING SERIOUS. IT CAN BE FRUSTRATING SEEING THEM WALK DOWN THE AISLE HAPPY WHILE YOU'RE MISERABLE. BUT SHACKING UP WITH SOMEONE WILL ALWAYS BE THE WRONG APPROACH, JUST TO KEEP YOUR APPEARANCE OF NOT BEING ALONE UP TO PAR. THE TRUTH IS, THE ONES WHO ARE MARRIED ARE FAR LONELIER THAN SOMEONE WHO IS SINGLE. GETTING MARRIED DOES NOT EQUATE TO INSTANT HAPPINESS, NEITHER IS IT SOMETHING TO DO JUST BECAUSE IT SOUNDS LIKE THE RIGHT THING TO DO; YOU MUST KNOW IT'S THE RIGHT THING TO DO FOR THE RIGHT REASONS.

DON'T SETTLE AND TRY TO BUILD LOVE

TRYING TO BRING SOMEONE YOU DO NOT LOVE INTO YOUR LIFE AND THINKING THAT YOU'LL EVENTUALLY LEARN HOW TO LOVE HIM OR HER NEVER REALLY WORKS OUT. CHANCES ARE, IF YOU'RE NOT INTO HIM OR HER RIGHT OFF THE BAT, YOU'RE

Not Settling for Less

PROBABLY NOT GOING TO BE INTO THEM IN THE FUTURE. NO RELATIONSHIP IS PERFECT, BUT IF YOU DON'T HAVE SOME SORT OF LOVE SOMEWHERE IN YOUR HEART, IT'S GOING TO BE HARD TO FORCE YOURSELF INTO HAVING SOME.

DON'T EVER LET MATERIAL THINGS SUBSTITUTE FOR LOVE

SURE, EVERYONE LOVES THE FINER THINGS IN THE WORLD, BUT THERE IS A RIGHT AND A WRONG WAY TO GET THEM. YOU CAN WORK AND GET THINGS YOU DESIRE, OR YOU CAN SETTLE FOR SOMEONE JUST BECAUSE THEY HAVE THESE THINGS ALREADY. NEVER SETTLE FOR SOMEONE BASED ON MATERIAL THINGS BECAUSE THINGS DON'T ALWAYS LAST FOREVER, AND MATERIAL THINGS WILL BECOME A HINDRANCE TO FINDING TRUE LOVE

Important

Important

Important

This book was designed for women as well as men to help someone recognize certain issues that they may be going through in life and how to overcome these issues. There are many issues in life that people choose to deal with, when, in reality, they don't have to. Everyone deserves to be happy in one way or another, so this is a stepping-stone to what was once thought of as undoable. If there is someone in your life who is not making you happy, you have the right book.

What you get out of reading this book is up to you. It boils down to how much strength you must move past these weights that you have in your life. If you have nothing holding you back, this book will show you all the signs to look for to avoid them. So, you must understand how to spot and weed them out. Just like a farmer who goes in and removes the bad weeds and fruit from the good ones, you have to do the same thing. The only difference is, the weeds that you are weeding out paint themselves up to look like wonderful weeds, but

Not Settling for Less

with the right tools, you can still weed them out from the good ones, and this book will help you do so.

No one deserves to put up with nonsense, and the good thing is that you don't have to. For this to work, you must admit that you are putting up with nonsense, and then you should take the steps to remove it. If you are in a relationship, and you're not happy, you're always arguing and fighting, you're always getting lied to and cheated on, then you have the right to move on and be happy. But it's up to you to do so. So, admit and remove!

Table of Contents

Not Settling for Less

What's something that I will not be doing?

Not Settling for Less
Better Believe It

You talk a good game

Everything that you say seems to be like no other

But, in all reality, it's hiding behind cover

Like a mask that Spider-Man dares not to remove

Words paint such a wonderful picture

But if a director cannot bring them to life

They only become just words, and nothing more

A killer only becomes a killer once they have drawn their

weapon

Someone only becomes a psychopath once they are

diagnosed

A hunter only becomes a hunter once they have shot

something worth keeping

Some of the most wonderful things in life

Only become wonderful when you decide they are worth

the sight

Settling

So, why should I settle for anything less?

Why should I accept all those lies?

Why should I accept all your abuse?

Why should I accept being second to another?

If I was to count every time you broke my heart

One may say, why waste your time with another?

Because nothing in life is a waste

It only becomes a waste when you don't learn from it

It's easy to give up

It's also easy to make a choice

But it gets hard when you have to live with it

The most wonderful things in life are the hardest things to

keep

So, as long as it's worth the keep

You will never have to

Settle for less

And it will never become a waste

Part 1

Part 1

Settling

Settling

Settling

To put firmly into a desired position or place

(*Established*)

When you settle, you tend to put someone unworthy into a position they don't deserve. Then they grow comfortably happy, while you're left miserable. Settling only brings dead weight into your life when you don't need it. When you settle, all you do is give your happiness away. Just think about it; most likely, the person you're settling for isn't what you truly want in your life, but you still settle because you're hoping he or she will become or change into what you truly desire. They may receive everything they desire, but what about what you desire? A person can only get a position in your life if you allow them to have it. So, if you really decide to allow them, just make sure they are worth it.

Not Settling for Less

Why People Settle

There are many reasons why someone chooses to settle. Whether it's because they are tired of being alone, or they're trying to keep a good appearance (trying to impress the world). It could be for money, status, or even wanting something that's not theirs. Whatever the case may be, just know that YOU DON'T HAVE TO SETTLE. There are plenty of good women, as well as good men, who have settled at one point or another in their lives, and most likely, they became single afterward, or they still are trying to hang on to something unworthy and have grown tremendously unhappy. You can only be as happy as you allow yourself to be, and your happiness is reflected through whomever you allow in your life.

Settling

Stuff People Settle For

The biggest thing that people settle for is money. I know everyone has heard the saying "Money can't buy you love"; that's because it can't. Money can only become something like a bandage; it covers up what's underneath—your true feelings. The only thing money is good for is creating other problems, the more money you have, the more things you have to do. Money doesn't have the power to create or buy the feeling of love. Money becomes something that you regret loving, something like a pill you have to take for a health issue. It's something you need to survive, but you hate the fact that it has that much control over your life. Status is something else someone settles for. They find someone who is established so that they can say he or she is the partner (trophy).

Not Settling for Less
The Difference between Settling and Not Settling

Settling is for a purpose that doesn't include the option of true happiness. When you're doing something and don't have an idea why, and you don't share that true connection of happiness, you won't have satisfaction in your life. Not settling is the total opposite; you have found the one that you can't live without for all the right reasons. You haven't fallen for the okey-dokey or anything that doesn't show prosperity. You will know the difference when you're truly happy, with no guilt to linger on or any red flags that you chose to look over or accept.

Accepting

The only way someone's excuses can continue to work is if you accept them every time they are thrown your way. Someone can only get away with something if you allow him or her to, the keyword being '**allow.**' You will become "a fool once, a fool twice, a fool once more" if you

Settling

allow it. Some don't have a caring bone in their body. If things are going their way, they will act like your best friends—as long as you continue to accept all the excuses that they throw your way. Try not to accept and you will see how many friends you thought were your friends disappear like a thief in the night right along with the one you thought was there because they loved you. A kind heart is everyone's treasure, but you must figure out who's worthy and who's not.

Making Up Excuses for Them

It takes courage, guts, and a great deal of character for someone to say that they messed up or, even more importantly, that they are sorry for it. Shifting blame or trying to throw camouflage over the mistake comes from a place of being prideful—and maybe even a little cowardice. Why people are so afraid of being human is beyond me. Another area where excuses can trip people up is when they use them to keep from doing something, achieving something, or growing in a particular area. If the excuse is legitimate

Not Settling for Less

(medical or physical), then it's not really an excuse as much as it is reality. Everyone has their character; how they choose to act is a choice of theirs, just like choosing to make excuses for everything. Making up excuses isn't fair to you, so do not allow them.

Letting Money Substitute for Love

Some people get so caught up in what someone can do or is doing for them—to the point that the whole relationship revolves around just that. Money becomes a substitution for what matters—love. Once someone gets comfortable with receiving money, that's all they see. So, at that point, they can care less about love, even though money can only get you so far. Money can't kiss you like you want to be kissed; it can't hug you the way you want to be hugged. Money surely can't love you the way you want to be loved, seeing that it shows no emotions, neither can it listen and respond to you venting after a frustrating day. The only

Settling

thing money is good for is buying things that never last, like a car that will break down eventually or jewelry that never shines like the first day you bought it. Money stays behind once you pass away, and it doesn't remember you when you're gone. So, don't become another lost soul manipulated by the things of the world. Learn to love things that truly matter, like family, friends, and people who care about you just as much as you care about them.

Real Love

Love is something special that's shared between two people—when you think about someone when you wake up and before you go to sleep. Love is something you can't see, but you can feel it. Real love is shared between two individuals, not one person who's head over heels with someone, and the other person is using that to keep one in a relationship with them, not caring for them in the same manner. When two people can build a love that no one can interfere with, then that's genuine love. Just know how to distinguish when it's real, like when someone is willing to put in just as much effort as you. That shows they are there to keep you happy just as much as you are. When someone doesn't care about your feelings and only cares about what you can do to make him or her happy, that's not real love; it's an imitation.

Things That You Let People Get Away With

You will never have control over what someone says or does, but you have control over whether someone says or does it to you or not. If someone is disrespectful, you have two outlets: you can either deal with it or not. If you deal with it (mental or physical abuse), most likely it is going to be an ongoing thing and isn't going to stop—just because you let them slide that time. If someone gets away with something once, they're going to think that they can get away with it again. If you deal with it and put your foot down, you're not settling for less. There will always be disrespectful individuals, but on the other hand, there will always be just as many respectful ones too. So, whatever it

Settling

is that you're thinking about letting someone get away with before you decide, you should ask yourself "Will it be worth it in the long run?" because you play a big part in your relationship when someone mistreats you or does something you dislike. You may not be able to change them, but you can surely change your relationship by making any changes you see fit.

Romantic Movie

How do I get you to see?

Romantic Movie
So, take notes

Picture waking up to breakfast in bed

Complimented by a rose and a letter

Flooded with feelings that arose from thoughts of

you

Picture yourself in my arms

As I kiss you, loving you, while I'm holding you

As I fall deep into your eyes

While the candlelight accompanies me with a

dance

Picture me stuck in your mind as you share a night

Watching the stars shoot across the sky

Lullabies of a perfect key played through a perfect

song

Dirty knees from asking a question of eternity

A scene that no one seems to forget

A green screen filled with stars as bright as your

Settling

smile

Which the camera can't seem to shoot past

A romantic movie like no other, starring you

A film shot by yours truly

Capturing all the moments that lovers share

Tied up in a bow, frozen in time

So, we can share for the rest of our lives

Part 2

Part 2

<u>Not Settling</u>

Not Setting

Not Settling

Not letting a person, place, or something into your life that will hinder your will to continue (*not letting true love cease to exist*)

By not settling, you are claiming happiness. You need to have a positive outlook on life to attract positive prospects to your life. Not settling isn't something easy to do, but it's doable. Once you give up on something so simple in life (settling), it only opens doors to other negative ventures. While dating, it takes time to learn someone, so learn them before handing them keys to unlock certain areas in your life. You hold the power and always have, so stand up for your heart because no one else will. If you are settling, it's your right not to, so don't. Nip it in the bud while you can so that you can stop the roots from growing out of control. The more you let it grow, the uglier it will become.

Not Settling for Less

Never Falling for Excuses

You're always going to run into problems in life, but if you run across someone who uses excuses for everything, then find someone who doesn't. A lot of excuses substitute for lies if you haven't met someone because they are always busy, or they have to work, or their car isn't working, etc. They keep feeding you excuses as a way to avoid you (people make time for what they want to make time for). One, they either have something to hide, or two, they are not who they claim to be. Some people in the world can sell you a dream and make it as believable as a card trick in Vegas. You get lured into a world of excuses. They will continue to use excuses to feed you whatever story they want—just to get whatever they want from you or to avoid you for however long they can, but that's only if you allow them to. So, don't start because once you do, you're only digging yourself into a deeper and deeper hole that you have to try and get out of.

Not Settling

Married Men/Women

Marriage is something special that should only be shared between two people. Not two people and a mistress or two people and a Mr. It's supposed to be until death does you part, not until someone comes in between. Married men/women sometimes tend to stray away from the true meaning of marriage and start to let other things interfere with their marriage. If you are having problems in your marriage, that's something you should work on with your partner or try to have marriage counseling so you can locate the issues in your marriage and work on them. When a married person finds someone who will become his or her mistress or Mr., it's because they have found someone to manipulate to give them what they want (usually something their wife or husband isn't doing) and still be able to do so without their wife or husband finding out. Even if their husband or wife were to find out, it doesn't make it OK for the mistress or Mr. to continue what he or she is doing.

Not Settling for Less

Just like the others who have heard "I'm getting a divorce" or "We are separated, but we just haven't got a divorce yet." Well, here is some free advice: they're not going to leave their wife or husband. For one thing, there is too much invested in their marriage to just walk away for someone they only intended to be there for the time being because you were the only one who fell for their story (game) in the first place. Next, do they even love you? Or do they just love what you allow them to get away with while they're with you? Don't settle for someone else's husband or wife when you can have your own.

God didn't stop making wives, and he surely didn't stop making husbands when he made theirs. Besides, you don't want to settle for someone who is sneaking out on his or her husband or wife. If they are sneaking out on them, what's going to make you so special that they won't sneak out on you? If you want to be blessed with your husband or wife, don't think you're going to receive that blessing when you're in between two people that God put together. How do you think God will bless you when you're destroying

Not Settling

something that he put together? The only thing you're doing is blocking your blessing.

Fake Love

Finding out if someone loves you or loves the fact of you is a coin toss. If someone is more worried about what you're going to do for them, rather than spending time with you; if someone cares about your money more than you, then they don't love you; they just love what you can do for them. There are plenty of people in the world who have become masterminds at using others. Some people have been alone for so long or have grown lonely, so when these sorts of people come into their lives, they accept them, for they feel some company is better than no company. If you think someone is showing you fake love, then cut off some of the things you do, like giving them money or always buying them stuff or catering to their every need. The reason is that if you cut off those things they want, they will show their true intentions.

Not Settling for Less
Don't Become Anyone's Keeper

It's not your job to take care of anyone; you shouldn't have to start off any relationship doing every little thing for someone. You shouldn't have to pay anyone's rent, car note, cable bill, insurance, cell phone bill, light bill, gas bill, or any other bill when you are getting to know them. If you are treating someone to dinner or a movie, that's one thing, but don't become someone's keeper. Once you start, that's what you're going to be doing forever. Furthermore, if you've never met someone in person, it's not advisable to start a relationship by spending money on someone who hasn't even spent quality 'face-to-face' time with you. Don't fall for excuses on why he or she can't spend time with you, because people make time for what they choose to make time for. If someone isn't spending time with you, they are spending time with someone else. So, if their conversation begins with "I'm stressing out" or "If this doesn't get paid," then it's not worth your time because that's all you're going to become—their keeper.

Not Settling
Don't Lower Your Standards

If you have standards, don't lower your standards for anyone (only for yourself). If you're not being too successful in the dating game, just re-evaluate your standards and adjust them because some people seem to set unrealistic standards that no one can live up to. But if you choose to re-adjust them, do it because you want to, and not because someone is getting your attention; and you're trying to make a good impression because, in the long run, they're going to do or say something that is going to trigger a red flag on your 'standards list.' If you don't know how to set standards, we will address that a little later on; but when you do start to set standards just keep them realistic and obtainable. Just remember that you may think that it is easy to do because it's something that you may be able to do, but in all reality, no one is you.

Not Settling for Less
Don't Become a Bank

If you want to give away free money, don't you think someone is willing to take it? Some people have mastered the skill of getting money from others. The people who stand on the corner with signs make a lot of money; they figure out what story they can use to make someone give them money, and they realize that their story is convincing enough for someone to help them out. Throughout the entire day, they can hustle up a few hundred dollars, if not more. Some people have gotten so good at it that begging for money has become their full-time job. If they can do it, then someone who has gotten you to invest your feelings into them can, with the right words, and have you investing more than just feelings. Becoming a bank isn't necessarily giving someone money; they can also get you to purchase things regularly for them. You have those who are good enough to manipulate someone out of money, and you have the ones who are good enough to get you to pay something for them (light bill, car note, gas bill, insurance, etc.) or buy them gifts (clothes, jewelry, shoes, etc.). But it's always your choice if you fall for it or not.

Don't Take Your Kindness for a Weakness

There are a lot of kind-hearted people, and there will always be someone who will try to take that kindness for weakness. For the longest time, the word 'No' wasn't in my vocabulary. But the more I didn't use the word 'No,' the more people would seem to come back time after time. Some with good intentions of paying me back or returning the favor, and others who cared less to return the favor but continued to have their hand out. So, as you can see, the word 'No' can be a valuable tool if you know how to use it. Just because you're a kind-hearted person doesn't mean that you have to let people run all over you. Don't let the word 'No' become the only word you know how to use but make it a word that makes your choices a little more meaningful. Who said you couldn't have a kind heart and still be a strong-willed person at the same time?

Not Letting Someone Become a Weight in Your Life

If there are certain goals that you have set in your life, don't let anyone interfere with them. Some people can come into your life and create weight in your life, either stopping or slowing down anything that you have put into motion. Once you feel that tug in your life, disconnect that anchor as soon as possible. There's nothing like having someone who is slowing you down from achieving goals in life. It mostly starts when they do not support what you're doing. Once that happens, they stray you away from your goals. Never give them that much power or control over your life. People who usually do this are people who don't have anything going for themselves.

Sympathy

How did I stay here so long?

Sympathy

But I deserve better

All the sneaking around

All the pain

All the rudeness

All the disrespect

Became a stiff pain of agony and sympathy

For the next person who you trick into believing

That you care for someone other than yourself, I

pity them

I used to think someone stole you from me

Then I realized that someone couldn't take

something that was never yours

From the start

I stressed about something that I had no control

over

I've witnessed a season that I've turned into a

lesson

Not Settling for Less

So, when there is a reason, I'll take it as a blessing

Time and time again I gave you another chance

But after enough time, any metal can begin to rust

After the waters of life take their course

Once I'm done

There's nothing more to be said or done

Because I have no reason to settle

Especially for someone who only lives for the seasons

So, I give you my sincere sympathy

Part 3

<u>Attraction</u>

Attraction

Attraction

The action or power of evoking interest, pleasure, or liking for someone or something (*Charm-Appeal-Attractiveness-Pull-Allurement*)

Many factors may influence one person's attraction to another, with physical aspects being one of them. In many cases, humans attribute positive characteristics, such as intelligence and honesty, to physically attractive people without consciously realizing it. Attractions can range from looks to personality. The first thing that usually attracts someone is how someone looks. You can also be attracted to someone's scent as well as if they are well groomed, clean cut, as well as nicely dressed. Personality is a form of attraction, whether it's from a conversation you and that person are sharing or even catching something that someone may be sharing in another conversation.

A nice smile can be a form of attraction; a nice smile can say so many things about a person without them having

Not Settling for Less

to say a word. Just to name a few attractions, there are sexual, symmetry, body scent, generics, waist-to-chest, musculature, height, hairiness, skin color, facial features, breasts, buttocks, as well as eye color. For both men and women, there appear to be universal criteria of attractiveness both within and across cultures and ethnic groups.

When considering long-term relationships, men seem to place a higher emphasis on physical attractiveness in a partner than women do. People make judgments of physical attractiveness based on what they see and also on what they know about the person. Beauty is a word that takes attractiveness to another level because beauty lures someone in, but nowadays, beauty doesn't get people too far; seeing that it takes more than beauty to have a healthy relationship. An attractive person is just the beginning; the next step is finding out if they are as beautiful on the inside just as much as they are on the outside.

Attraction
Looks

Attraction is a big deal when it comes to a relationship, but people always pass up someone or something based on how it looks. Someone can be the most genuine person, and just because you might have seen him or her out and about in shorts and a t-shirt, you tend to pass them up (which becomes a mistake on your end). In most cases, people have certain features that they would like someone to have: light skin, six-pack, muscular, dreads, long hair, dark skin, tall, short, low fade, etc. Looks are a form of attraction, but some tend to overdo it. They want someone with all these features as well as a good heart. Sometimes you can't have this perfect person that you're painting in your head. Just learn how to keep your expectations realistic. Being realistic is something that most can't seem to do.

Not Settling for Less

The Heart

There are people that are really genuine and loving, but there is only one way to learn how someone's heart is, and that's by talking and getting to know them. There's so little you can learn about someone just from a short conversation. People nowadays are so good at hiding who they truly are, but time shows all and reveals everything. The heart is a special thing, but you have to find that special person who is willing to take care of your heart and comfort it the way it should be cherished. Not everyone takes care of your things the way you do or the way you would like them to, but there is always someone who will. So, never lose hope.

Respect

You have to respect yourself for someone else to respect you. If you act or talk a certain way, just know you

Attraction

attract what your spirit gives off. If you dress a certain way, people tend to approach you based on the vibe you give off. The best way to get respect is to give it. Most people expect to receive respect from someone just because they feel they deserve it. You have to be willing to give respect just as much as you want to get it. Respect is given where it is due; if it's not due, then you will not receive it. Respect can be a specific feeling of regard for the actual qualities of the one respected, e.g., "I respect her judgment." *Respect* sometimes is confused with tolerance since tolerance doesn't necessarily imply subordination to one's qualities but means treating others as equal. They are easily misinterpreted.

Someone with a Job

How can you expect someone to do for you when they can't do for themselves? It's different if someone has always had a job, and they ran across some hard times. If someone doesn't have determination, how can you expect

Not Settling for Less

him or her to want to even get a job, let alone keep it? When you run across someone who has had a job for a while and is looking for a new one, that's reasonable, but never having a job and isn't looking, you may want to think twice before you make an exception.

Someone Who Has Goals

It's always reassuring to know someone is trying to better themselves in one way or another. If someone is trying to better themselves, they are most likely willing to do what it takes to better their relationship. If you're trying to have something in life, your best bet is to have someone who wants more out of life as well. If you want the same ole thing, then get someone who does the same ole thing. You can't expect to build something with someone who doesn't want anything in life. Some people are satisfied with the normal nine to five, while others are trying to go above and beyond. Just don't get stuck in a relationship where you're the only one going beyond.

Attraction
Character

Everyone has different characteristics that set him or her apart from others. Those are the things that catch someone's attention. They can come off as a genuine person or even someone with a divine sense of humor. They can also come off as outgoing or caring, but it is your job to home in on what sparks your interest. Some people come off as bossy or controlling; these are things that help you distinguish one person from another. Here is a list of different personal characteristics: Achievement, Deference, Orderliness, Exhibition, Autonomy, Affiliation, Sensitiveness, Neediness, Dominance, Abasement, Nurturance, Change, Endurance, Heterosexuality, and Aggression, just to name a few. These are all the most common personal characteristics that help you distinguish who a person is without even having to ask them. How someone acts will tell you all you need to know about them, whether they are just around you or around a group of people. Some people are more outgoing than others; while others like more attention, so they stand out. Then you have

Not Settling for Less

the total opposite, someone who needs attention, but they don't know how to get it. Some try to distinguish everyone's feelings by trying to put themselves in someone else's shoes, trying to figure out what works for them and what fits into their perfect lives. Just remember, everyone can't fit into everyone's life. If he or she could, there would be no need to date because everyone would be satisfied.

Silky Petals
How can I describe you?

Silky Petals
So Perfect

The silky feeling of rose petals

Could never fathom the true sensation of your lovely skin

An attraction stimulated by touch

With a look of a finer blend of pure chocolate

A woman in a league, all of her own

A sight that manipulates eyes and captures forever

Stuck in the moment as if you've seen heaven for the first

time

The silky petal of life that covers your body

As if you were wrapped in a silky sheet

That was tightened until every curve of your body was

defined

As if the silky petals were painted on your body

After dipped in chocolate

Captivating and luscious mixed together

Which creates 'Magnificent'

Silky petals, a creation like no other

Not Settling for Less

To symbolize a woman like no other

Through my eyes, I see a sight like no other

When distance reflects, makes me miss you like no other

As I wait to glide my fingers across your silky petals that

are like no other

Silky Petals

Part 4

<u>Factors</u>

Factors

Factors

(A circumstance, fact, or influence that contributes to a result or outcome)

Many factors are placed in our lives; both good and bad. Anything that results in factors in our life creates an outcome. Many factors will be placed in your life, but you have to choose between them and what will produce the best outcome for your life. Not everyone is made for everyone; this is why these different factors will help you decide circumstances that you're willing to accept into your life. The fact of the matter is that you deserve to be happy so "do just that." Life is like a puzzle, and it's your job to place the correct pieces in the correct places. So, choose fact or fiction. Fact is reality, and fiction is something that resembles something perfect, but in all reality, "nothing is perfect."

Not Settling for Less

Lines

You must be able to distinguish between someone who is a master at telling you everything you want to hear, and someone that is telling you what you need to hear. A person will come up with the best lines in the world to get what they want. They say practice makes perfect, and these lyrical people practice their craft. Even Michael Jordan didn't become phenomenal overnight. One way to tell if someone is just trying to pull a fast one is if they don't remember anything that you both have talked about. They may be able to remember a few things, but every dog has its day. You want someone who wants to hear what you have to say, not someone who doesn't even care about your well-being. It's best to know where you're headed so that you can find someone else who is headed in the same direction.

Factors
Self-esteem

How can someone make you happy when you're not happy with yourself? Some people have been put down so much that their self-esteem is low. Put-downs like telling you that you will never be anything in life or that you're not beautiful, your fat, or even too skinny. If your self-esteem is constantly being abused, all the time, you have the power to change all of that. You can look in the mirror and tell yourself that you are beautiful. You must be happy with yourself and not care about what others think of you. If they can't love you for who you are, then they're not worth your time. If someone can't love you for who you are, there is always someone willing to.

Being Hurt

Everyone has been hurt at one point or another in his or her life. They always say that one bad apple can spoil the bunch—not if you remove it. Don't let anyone affect your future.   You will never find true love if you're holding onto

Not Settling for Less

your past. If someone is in your past, they are there for a reason. You will never know when you're going to run into Mr. or Mrs. Right. Most take being hurt hard instead of just taking it how it truly is—and that is, taking that experience and learning from it. Just think about it; if you never went through things in life, you wouldn't be the person you are today. Most don't embrace what they go through, but that's what makes you a better person. It trains you to know how to handle similar situations, making you more knowledgeable and more of a well-rounded individual. You have to learn to embrace hurt and channel it into a positive outlook.

Control

Being controlling is a big problem in relationships. Once someone uses scare tactics and abuse, they trap someone into believing that there is no way out; when in all reality, there is always a way out. You just have to want a way out and find it. You can google anything nowadays and

Factors

find the answers to questions you may have. It's just the fear of thinking that no one can help you or the fear of being alone. Just remember there is always help for any and every situation. It's better to be alone than to be controlled. A person can only get away with things that you allow to happen.

They will continue to get away with these things for as long as you allow it. There is verbal abuse and physical abuse, where the abuser will form a sense of fear that opens a door to constant control over someone. If you are in control of a plane, and the system malfunctions, then you're stuck with no control whatsoever.

The same thing lies within a relationship. If you take away control from someone, his or her power ceases to exist. Never give someone that much power over you to the extent that they control everything that you do or say. Getting out of an abusive relationship isn't easy. You may wish time will change things, or you're scared of what your partner may do if you try to leave.

Whatever it may be, you probably feel trapped and helpless. There are plenty of resources available for verbal and physical abuse. Don't ever feel that you are to be

Not Settling for Less

blamed for their actions. You deserve to be treated with respect just like any other human being. Here are a few help options: In the US, call the **National Domestic Violence Hotline at 1-800-799-7233**. You can also visit the **International Directory of Domestic Violence Agencies** for a global list of helplines, shelters, and crisis centers. In the UK, call **Woman's Aid at 0808 2000 247**. In Canada, call the **National Domestic Violence Hotline at 1-800-363-9010**.

What You Put Off

The things that you wear create a certain aura around you. If a woman dresses more educated, she's going to be approached differently than a woman wearing shorts, with her butt hanging out the bottom. A business-looking woman is more likely to be approached with more respect than a woman who doesn't even respect herself. There could be a very educated man who may have gone to the store with shorts on that might have been a tad big and could be sagging just a little; he could try to approach a

Factors

woman, but she might turn him down just for the fact that he is sagging his pants. However, that same man could have walked into the store with a suit, looking more professional, and could have approached the same woman; where she may most likely give him a little more time and have a conversation. Your appearance plays a big part in how far you get in life; if you're presentable, you will likely be taken more seriously. Most people become hypocrites because they want to be approached and respected, but they leave the house with booty shorts and a tight shirt, showing everything. Most likely you're going to attract guys who have one thing on their mind, and it's not going to be making you his one and only, unless he's into that kind of thing. And if he is, that says a lot about what type of man he is.

Not Settling for Less
Setting Standards

Life is not a chore to endure; it is an opportunity for fun, self-expression, personal growth, and representing something people can respect. Setting standards isn't a bad thing; you should have some kind of standards in life that you live by that others can respect as well. If you allow someone to disrespect you, they will do just that. If you let someone call you outside of your name, they will continue to call you outside of your name. Setting standards is as easy as meaning what you say and living by it. You can start with little things such as someone who has a job, car, or his or her place; someone respectful; someone who has good hygiene; someone with goals; whatever makes you happy. Don't set standards that are almost impossible to achieve. Not everyone cares if someone has a car, but they may at least want someone to have a job. Not everyone cares if someone has his or her own place, but they may want someone respectful. I'm pretty sure you get the picture. Build your standards around who you are and what's going to be appealing to you. Whatever your standards may be,

Factors

just ensure that you set some, whether big or small. Just be open-minded and know that no one is perfect, and they might not be able to meet every single thing that you may have on your list. If there is something that's small, it doesn't hurt to let something 'small' pass. Someone could have a car, a job, and his or her own place, but they are disrespectful; that's not something that you want to pass on. Just know yourself and what you want.

When Enough Is Enough

There will always be a time when you have to put your foot down and stop something that may be driving you crazy or even something that you are allowing to alter your life. Whatever your "enough" is, just make sure you stop it before it pushes you over the edge. You should never have to feel miserable in a relationship. You deserve to be in a relationship that was built on a good foundation and is continuing to grow for the good. If you're getting abused mentally or physically, you're well overdue for true happiness, and you need to find a way out before it's too

Not Settling for Less

late. You should start to dream of a happy life and start working towards that life. The first step to having a happy life is to know that you have put up with enough. Then, get a plan together to get out of the situation. Finally, suck up those mixed feelings and move on so you can share something special with someone who cares to share it with you. Are you tired of being in someone's bank? Are you tired of being second to another man or woman? Are you tired of being put down for any and everything? Well, are you? If the answer is yes, then you have reached the stage where enough is enough. If you are thinking this, then the answer is probably yes. If you're happy, then you won't have to ever think twice; you will just know you're happy.

People Make Time for What They Want to Make Time For

Just think about it; if you have kids or a job and you want to go out, what do you do? You see when you can get a babysitter so that you can go out and enjoy yourself. Just

Factors

like you have to make plans to go out, someone else can make time as well. It doesn't matter the situation, there is always a solution. A solution is only acquired by those who makes the effort to find it; if someone wants to see you, they will. Excuses only go so far; not everyone will make up excuses, so be able to distinguish between the two. If you have talked to someone for a month or two months, and you asked to meet up with them six or more times, and you haven't met them, most likely you won't; so, move on. If someone isn't making time for you, then they are making it for someone else.

Want Their Cake and Ice-Cream

This is a term you may be familiar with, and for those who don't know what it means, pretty much want your girl and a girl on the side or your man and a man on the side. The world has changed in many ways, and this particular saying has taken a toll on many people's lives. There are millions of reasons why people do what they do. But it doesn't

Not Settling for Less

matter why they do it. All that matters is that you don't have to be second to anyone.

Everyone deserves to be with someone they love and not have to worry about if he or she is messing around. Worrying only brings stress, and stress brings health problems. So, why accept or deal with something in your life that will cause fatigue and will wear and tear your body? You deserve better, so leave behind all the worry and move forward to someone worth your time.

Not everyone wants both desserts at once; some prefer one piece, and that is enough to satisfy them. It's better to have one anyway to savor the taste. So, wait for the one who will savor that one special taste. Just know you owe it to yourself to have someone in your life that will appreciate and respect you that much, to savor you for a lifetime. Stop settling and start enjoying your life because you only have one.

How Will I Know

Why are there so many thoughts in my head?

How Will I Know?

Follow the truth

So afraid to let you in

So many things running through my mind

Leaving me clueless like an amazing trick at the circus

Saying all the things that my heart aches for

So sincere and caring, so passionate and loving

But is this a real key to my heart or an imitation?

Could you really express love?

Or are you just a good painter?

Painting those beautiful skies that share a beautiful sunset

Over two hands swing as they share the moment

How will I know

If you are real or a cliché?

You may say all the things someone should say

You may do all the things someone should do

So tired of all the false hopes

So tired of all the lies

A dream reveals someone special

Factors

But the act of real brings them to life

So, make me give you all of me, then I will know

That my dreams don't deceive me

Part 5

Part 5

<u>Urban Novel</u>

Chapter 1

Early Morning Hours

It was 1:35 a.m. in the midnight hours. A cork sat on the cream rug all evening, leaving a slight stain on the cream plush carpet. A champagne bottle with a smug of liquor, which lingered in the bottom of a sparking glass container. A bottle left a trail of liquor that dampened the brown mahogany wood table, leaving a scent of delicate delight that engulfed the room like a fresh meadow of roses on a sunny summer day. A bucket that once contained ice had melted away, leaving behind a pool of refreshment after a long hot day.

The bucket of water had cascaded across the room so many hours back, creating a puddle of water that dripped off the table onto his tainted dress shoe. Strands of clothing were dashed around the room like a twister had dropped them off. A shirt here, some pants there, a top here, some

Not Settling for Less

lingerie there, a stocking here, a sock there. Like a striptease had completed its mission. An oozing bottle of whipped cream had joined the party as well. A topping of a strawberry delight was used to decorate and paint designs all over a plush stomach.

Foreplay with a hint of cream, leaving behind a sticky sweet surface. Rose petals decorated the floor like sprinkles on ice cream. Candles started to wither away from a continuous burn as the flames lingered softly to the right from the cool breeze of the air conditioner, causing the wax to ooze down the side of the remaining candlestick. The reflection from the TV created a collage that cascaded across the ceiling like a dark sunset. Body limbs stretch across the bed, intertwined like they were playing twister, partially covered by silky elegant sheets resembling an ancient painting, creating the illusion of nudity.

A sweet taste of a sinful desire that some welcome with open arms like a baby that was just brought into the world. Hair destroyed from an activity that created a hot passionate lust that pumped on like a steady-paced heartbeat. Subtle breaths of relief had settled in now that

Chapter 1

their bodies had finally begun to rest. She slides her right hand across his chest, softly caressing him.

His body reacted with a slight alteration of his position to the right, taking in a deep breath as he turned over. She snuggled up behind him as his body shifted to a new position. Cuddled up like a bear in hibernation, a sweet sensation of comfort.

Brendan's phone struck 2:00 a.m., and the alarm sounded off, a sound that grew louder and louder.

BEEP ...

BEEP ...

BEEP ...

BEEP ...

BEEP ...

The beeping continued, with less than a second pause between each beep. Brendan turned and slid his legs off the bed as he got untwined from Janae's arms and cut off the alarm. Janae opened her eyes slowly; her sight went from a cloudy blur to a sharp focus as she looked up at Brendan's muscular back, one that she couldn't help but rub her fingers

Not Settling for Less

across as she caressed him gently. Voice distorted from hours of vigorous, luscious, and delicate body encounters.

"Hey, you," Janae whispered as she lusted over his chocolate skin.

Brendan turned around and looked back at Janae as they smiled at each other.

"Hey, baby," said Brendan.

"Where are you going, baby?" Janae asked, even though she already knew the answer. She was just hoping that one day, it would change to appeal to her needs.

"Now, you know I have to go home," Brendan replied.

"Why can't you ever stay the whole night with me?" Janae asked, already quite aware of the answer—an answer that haunted her every time they met up.

"Now, you know why I can't stay; you act like this is something new," Brendan replied, tired of explaining the same thing over and over.

Smacking her lips, Janae said, "I know, but that's not fair. I want to have you to myself at least one full night."

"Soon you will have me all you want—once I take care of the situation. But you must be patient because it's not

Chapter 1

something that's going to happen overnight," said Brendan, feeling like a record that was skipping continuously.

"I know; it just bothers me sometimes. Seems like it's taking forever. It's already been 9 months. How much longer is it going to take?" Janae asked.

"I don't know, but I'm working on it. I'm going as fast as I can, there's only so much that I can do. All we can do right now is wait until it's all said and done," said Brendan.

"I hear you, but you need to get that taken care of," Janae replied.

"What do you think I'm doing? You're always in my face about this, but when I give you all these gifts, you don't have anything to say. Now, I'm trying to get it done.

I'm working on a couple of things with some of my property, and I'm trying to get my banking accounts sorted out. So have some patience," said Brendan.

"Ok, I will, dang. I'm just tired of waiting," Janae replied.

Brendan got up and walked around as he got his stuff together. He saw one of his shoes by the table, reaching down and grabbing it, damped from the water that dripped

Not Settling for Less

from the bucket of ice. "Damn, this bucket has my shoe soaking wet," he said as he grabbed a nearby towel and tried to dry his shoe a little. He looked up at Janae, saying, "My shoe is almost as wet as I got you last night."

With a slight grin on her face, Janae replied, "Whatever! Don't be trying to change the subject. I'm still mad at you."

"Girl, you know I Love You. Why are you acting like that?" Brendan asked.

Smiling, Janae replied, "Whatever! You don't love me. If you did, you wouldn't be leaving me now, would you?"

"Stop acting like that. Can you help me find my other shoe?" said Brendan as he looked around.

Wrapping herself in the sheet, Janae got out of bed, walked up by the TV, and grabbed Brendan's shoe from beside the TV. "Here it is," she replied.

"How did it get up there?" Brendan asked.

Smiling and biting her bottom lip, Janae said, "You know how crazy we get."

Shaking his head, Brendan walked over to grab the shoe from Janae, but she put it behind her back. "The only way you're getting this back is if you give me a kiss with those

Chapter 1

delectable lips. Mmm ...," she mumbled while holding his shoe tight in her hand.

Swiftly, Brendan reached and grabbed her hair, snatching her head gently to the right. Kissing her furiously, he said, "I'm trying to leave, so you need to go get back in bed before you start round 2."

Janae ran and jumped on the bed and replied, "Let's go."

"As nice as that sounds, I can't take you up on your offer this time. But I'll take a rain check," Brendan replied.

Not giving her the answer that her body cried out for, Janae whipped her head back on the bed, snatching the cover over her head. "Ugh," she grunted.

Brendan got all his stuff together and rushed into the bathroom to shower. He closed the bathroom door behind him. Janae got up and walked up to the door and asked, "Can I at least join you?"

Yelling through the door, Brendan replied, "Now, you know if you come in here, it's going to be more than a shower going on."

Not Settling for Less

"Whatever! Brendan, you're tripping," Janae replied, smacking her lips and getting back in the bed. She lay in the bed, listening to the water run as the steam poured from under the door, wishing she were in the bathroom with him. About 5 minutes later, the shower was cut off, and Brendan scrambled around in the bathroom, trying to get dressed. A text came through on Brendan's phone, which he had left on the side table next to the bed. Janae's eyes crept to the left and then back to the right, hoping Brendan didn't hear it. She slid over to the other side of the bed and grabbed his phone, picking it up.

Reading the display, she wanted to respond, so she began to enter four-digit numbers that she thought might be important enough for him to create a code. She entered his birth month and day, but the phone displayed "Access Denied." Then she entered his year of birth; the phone displayed "Access Denied." She thought deeply and hard; she knew that if she didn't get it right this time, it wouldn't let her try anymore. She remembered a date that he had mentioned before. So, she tried once more with that date, and the phone was unlocked. As soon as she tried to get to the messages, the bathroom door squeezed open. So, she

Chapter 1

hurried up and pushed the button to make the screen go dark, laid the phone back on the table, and rolled back over to her side of the bed.

Walking out of the bathroom, Brendan straightened up his tie. "Baby, I got to go," he said. Then he walked over, grabbed his phone, walked over, and kissed her on the forehead. "I'll give you a call later, OK?" he said.

Looking up at Brendan, slightly upset, Janae replied, "Ok."

Brendan placed the room's card on the table as he walked out. "Don't forget to turn in this card when you check out," he said as he exited the room.

"OK, I won't," Janae replied with a look of discomposure in her eyes.

Chapter 2

Chapter 2

Lurking

Brendan's bright lights illuminated the driveway as he pulled up and triggered the button to open the garage. He slowly crept in, parking slightly to the left of his wife's car. He grabbed his phone and put it on silent before he exited the car. The messages from Janae kept coming back-to-back like an orgasm that had gotten stuck and wouldn't go away. He looked up in his flip-down mirror so he could check his tie one more time before he entered his house. Stepping out of the car, brushing a little lent off his clothes, he unlocked the back door of his car and then grabbed his suitcase from the back seat. Proceeding to walk into the house, he reached over and hit the garage button on the wall as he walked in the door.

He walked in and looked around as the silence penetrated his soul. A lamp was on in the corner, so he was able to walk in without having to cut on any other lights. He

Not Settling for Less

headed straight for the kitchen and placed his suitcase on the counter; he walked over, opened the cabinet, and grabbed a glass to pour himself some champagne. Walking over, he opened the Frigidaire, grabbed a bottle out, and started to pour himself a glass full. Placing the bottle on the table, he tossed his glass up and took a big gulp. Just as he started to drop the glass down from his face, he looked up, and his wife was standing right in front of him.

"Hey, baby! What are you doing up so late?" Brendan asked.

"I was waiting up for you to make sure you got home safe. So, you must have had a long day at the office again?" Parris asked.

"Ya! You know it, baby. They be working your man to death," Brendan replied.

"Ya, I know. So, when is your vacation so we can get away and have some alone time, with no work, no phones, just me and you laid out on a beach somewhere?" Parris asked as she hugged Brendan around the neck, pressing her body against his.

Chapter 2

"It will be sooner than you think. I'm working on that. I'm ready to chill with my baby too," Brendan replied as he placed his hand on her waist.

"So, how was your day, sweetheart?" Parris asked, looking up into Brendan's eyes.

"It was OK, just busy. I'm happy to be off finally," said Brendan.

"Well, I'll cut on the shower for you, and I also cooked dinner for you. I made your favorite. Sheppard's pie and corn. So, you go grab something to wear and get in the shower, and I'll heat your plate," said Parris.

"OK. Wow! You did all that for your man! Thank you, sweetie! Wish I could have been here to eat dinner with you but had to stay in a little late," said Brendan.

"It's OK; I know you're handling business," Parris replied.

"See, that's just why I love you so much, and I made you Mrs. Jackson," said Brendan, kissing Parris. "Mwah!"

"And I'm happy to be Mrs. Jackson," Parris replied, smiling undeniably.

"You know what we haven't done in a while?" Brendan asked.

Not Settling for Less

Parris looked up at Brendan and asked, "What's that?"

"Well, you go ahead and get the shower together for me, and I'll meet you in there so I can show you," Brendan replied.

"OK, baby," said Parris.

As Parris walked away, Brendan smacked her on the butt; she turned around and softly bit her bottom lip.

"All right now, Daddy; don't start nothing you can't finish," said Parris.

"We are going to see who can finish something in a minute," Brendan responded.

Parris turned around and walked into the room. Brendan took out his phone and texted Janae "Goodnight!" Then he put the champagne back into the Frigidaire, grabbed his suitcase, turned out the lights, and walked into the room to get his nightwear together.

Finally, in the room, Brendan opened his dresser drawer and pulled his wallet out of his pocket. He placed it in his drawer and grabbed a pair of boxers and a tank top. Walking over to the closet, he took off his pants and his dress

Chapter 2

shirt, tossed them into the clothes hamper, and walked to the bathroom, not knowing that a wrapper was slightly leaning out of his pants pocket, shinning like a brand-new car straight off the lot, a destiny that not even a lie could camouflage because the truth will always come to light. Not even the deepest crevasse in the deepest cave can hide. Someone always finds what was once something that not even Brendan or Parris knew existed, but Parris would unravel the mystery.

Brendan walked into the bathroom and placed his clothes on the sink top as Parris stood there in some lingerie. "Oh, wow! That's how you feel?" Brendan asked.

"Well, I guess it looks that way," Parris replied.

Brendan walked up, grabbed Parris in his arms, and started kissing her soft and slow as if he was scared that he might break her. As he kissed her, thoughts of times that he and Janae shared ran through his head. How he kissed and hugged her the same way. Then he got more aggressive, pulling her hair and kissing her as if he was missing this in his marriage, not realizing that his thoughts started to come to life at that very moment. He grabbed his wife's hair and started going crazy, kissing her like she was fresh meat. He aggressively attacked her body like never before.

"Damn, baby! Slow down! We have plenty of time," Parris said as she embraced it and smirked slightly like she somewhat enjoyed it.

Not realizing it at first, Brendan finally snapped back to reality. He stopped and looked her in the eyes. "Umm, I'm sorry, honey. I don't know what came over me," he said, trying to overcome the awkward moment. "You just look so good. Dang it! Just made me feel like it was our first time all over again," he said while waiting for her to say something.

"Oh, is that right?" she said with a smile.

"Ummmhhh," Brendan replied.

"I see you still know what to say to get me all rallied up," Parris replied.

Taking a deep breath, Brendan went back in for another kiss. The steam from the shower started to engulf the bathroom like mist covering the cornfields after the morning dew had settled in. Steaming up the mirrors, the steam surrounded them like a cloudy heaven scene. Brendan was gently grazing his hands through her hair, softly

Chapter 2

kissing her neck as she softly rubbed her fingers around the back of his head.

"Yes ... Yes, baby ...," said Parris, for she was deep in the moment.

Brendan ran his hands down the back of her neck, across her shoulder blades, tickling her spine with his fingertips. He caressed her back ever so softly; the humidity from the steam dampened her lingerie to the point where it started to grip her body.

"You know you have to come out of this, right?" Brendan whispered in her ear.

"Oh, is that right?" Parris whispered back.

"Yes, it is," Brendan replied, sliding his hands down her waist, down further to the delicate lacing that trimmed and swirled just below her waist. He placed his fingertips under the trimming, grasping her thighs snugly, then releasing them as he gazed into her eyes and slid his hands up. The higher he got, the hotter the situation got as he guided her lingerie over her head and then dropped it to the floor. He slid his boxers off as he pulled her close, forcing his body toward her, causing her to step back until her heel pressed against the tub. Reaching over, he pulled the curtain

Not Settling for Less

back, and they both stepped into the shower and let the water cleanse their bodies, dripping and flowing down and around the curves and crevasses that sunlight dared not approach. Brendan continued to kiss her all over as the water chased his lips around like a cheetah on a gazelle. Moans skipped to the lou across the moist tiles throughout the room.

"I've been waiting for you all day," Parris said as she softly moaned in his ear.

"I can say the same thing," Brendan replied as he slid his right hand down her stomach, down to her right inner thigh, and around to the back of her thigh, slowly lifting her thigh as he curled her leg in his arm. He pressed her to the wall, holding her right butt cheek tight. He slid up in between her juicy lips, penetrating her womanhood. She swiftly grasped his back tight—to the point that her fingers almost indented his back as if she were squeezing a plush pillow.

"Ummmmm ...," Parris moaned as she absorbed his strokes. She symbolized them as a strong and sensational love, a love that can only be constructed through the vows of marriage. But the intention of greed was starting to take its

Chapter 2

toll. He penetrated through her skin with a very gentle kiss, a very comforting hug, with every stroke into her depths of love only speeding up its course. In and out, he stroked, pressing her body up against the wet tile, loving her like he was escaping the cage of virginity. He was trying to conquer every corner of her body as if he were giving her an examination. Her body was so wet, but there wasn't a clear view because their love just washed right down the drain as the water ran the lovemaking away. The deeper he got, the closer she pulled him near, and the tighter he gripped her ass. Holding her thighs firmly, he lifted her up and down, taking her on the ride of her life. Her skin kept sounding off every time their bodies collided; that created a feeling that forced a reaction of affection. Her body couldn't help but respond to the situation which had arisen.

"Shitttt ... Damn, baby ...," Parris screamed as she wrapped her hands around the back of his head, holding on for the ride. That moment seemed like the ride of her life. Brendan had almost reached the point of no return, feeling as if the sky was the limit. His body had come to the point where it was starting to grow weak; all of his energy was headed toward his organs.

Not Settling for Less

"Damn, baby! I'm about to cum," Brendan muttered.

Kinetic energy seemed to fluctuate between them like a chain reaction. Down her spine, the energy traveled.

"Me, too, baby!" Janae screamed. She made him feel as if he had the power to shoot to Mars.

Brendan eased her down slowly as he grabbed his treasure that sprinkled all over her gems. "Ohhhhhh ... Shit!" Brendan screamed, shivering as the water washed him a clean slate. He was stuck for a few seconds, trying to gain his composure. Parris stroked his back, but the timing was off because the tender moment caused him to jolt. He felt all fuzzy inside while the warm water heated the once-cold vessel. After his body had gained its composer, Brendan got out of the shower, dried off, and pulled back the curtains; then he grabbed her towel and opened it up so he could wrap her in it. "Here you go, baby," said Brendan.

"Thank you, honey," Parris replied, stepping out of the shower as her husband wrapped her up nicely and snugly.

Brendan walked out of the bathroom with her, climbed on the bed, and laid back; then, he reached over and

Chapter 2

cut on the lamp while Parris climbed on the bed and placed her head on his chest.

"I love you, baby," said Parris, while looking into Brendan's eyes.

"I love you too," Brendan replied. Kissing her on the forehead, he slowly ran his fingers through her hair and then down to her back, rubbing her back in a circular motion, looking down at her as she lay there like an angel, with her eyes closed, resting on his chest. The soft light grazed across her skin like the morning light peeping through the window blinds. As they both lay there, with the towel draped over their bodies, Brendan thought to himself, *how ungrateful am I! I have a great woman, but my sex addiction won't let me rest!* An addiction that he had grown too scared to bring up to his wife because he was afraid of the troubles that it would bring. Too ashamed to visit a therapist, the pride that would keep him as a prisoner for as long as breath circulated through his body. So, he sucked it up and enjoyed a marriage that was getting surrounded by lies. A marriage that could only be altered by time.

Deep in thought, Brendan glanced over at his phone and noticed that a message had come through. He looked up

Not Settling for Less

at the clock; the time was 3:04 a.m. Looking down at Parris, not wanting to wake her, he gradually leaned over to reach for his phone on the nightstand. Parris altered her position slightly and forced Brendan to freeze in his tracks. After she had settled, he gently held her head and slid to the right from underneath her slowly. Finally standing to his feet, he stood there to make sure she was still asleep. Seeming like the coast was clear, he walked around the bed, grabbed his phone, cut off the light, tip-toed out of the room, and headed to his office. While he crept out of the room, Parris opened her eyes, not moving a muscle as the light from the door dimmed down to a withering nothing as he slowly shut the door. Walking into his office, he gently closed the office door behind him. Sitting down in his chair, he turned on his computer, leaned back, and checked his phone. Looking down, he noticed that the message was from Janae.

"I can't sleep. I miss you already," Janae texted.

"Miss you too," Brendan replied. He laid his phone down on his desk face-up as he waited for his computer to boot up. A couple of seconds had passed, and his computer

Chapter 2

finally was completely booted; he heard a slight knock on his office door. He looked up as Parris walked into his office.

"Baby, why are you still up?" Parris asked, looking at the clock on his desk. "Baby, it's late, and you know you have to be up early," she added.

"Just have something that I must finish by tomorrow. Why? Are you OK?" Brendan asked.

"Yes, I'm fine. Just hurry up and come back to bed," said Parris.

"I will, baby. Be in there in a sec," said Brendan. Glancing down at his phone, he noticed that Janae was texting him back, so he grabbed some papers on his desk and covered his phone with them. "Dang! I don't know what I did with that paper," said Brendan.

"You need some help finding it?" Parris asked with a suspicious look on her face.

"No, baby; I got it. Go get some rest. I'll find it. I just had it," Brendan replied as he shuffled his papers around on his desk.

"OK. Good night," Parris said as she walked out of Brendan's office.

Not Settling for Less

Brendan waited a couple of seconds to make sure Parris was gone before he searched for his phone under the papers that he had scattered across the desk. Looking at the text that Janae had sent, "Can't wait to see you again," Brendan smiled, unaware that Parris was right outside the door, peeking through the slender crack as he groaned with delight. Not wanting to know who was on the other side of the phone, Parris walked off toward the bedroom.

Chapter 3

Tested Positive

Tuesday, the following day, Parris was at her job at the clothing retail store, where she was the store manager, and she was on her lunch break, enjoying lunch with one of her close friends, Michelle. It was a beautiful day to sit outside for a meal of delight. The sky was painted blue like it was straight off a canvas. Birds glided through the sky like a Disney movie, minus the ratings. People rushed by as if they all were late for an important meeting. Cars flew down the street as the sound of their engines paned back and forth from building to building, down alleys, and up crevasses. Crevasses that had been encrypted throughout the years of man's existence; the smell of the café had played with the emotions of passing peasants. The scent created an urgency to stop, but it hurt souls because the day already had locked in times for daily duties. Parris had become one of the victims, but time was in her favor. They were outside, relaxing at the seductive restaurant of many smells called Silverado's.

"Girl, thanks for coming out here to have lunch with me. Brendan was supposed to have joined me for lunch, but he said something came up at the office, so he won't be able to make it. This man and that job! It doesn't seem like he ever has time for me anymore," said Parris.

"It's OK, girl. That's why you have your girl. I always got your back," Michelle replied.

"Ya, I know … Don't know what I would do without you sometimes," said Parris.

"Good thing you don't have to do anything without me because I love these free meals. Brendan needs to cancel with you more often," Michelle laughed.

"Oh, really? I don't know what you're going to do when I start making you pay for your own food," Parris replied.

"So, you're going to do me like that?" Michelle replied.

Chapter 3

"You know I got you. But your butt is going to have to start paying for your food sometimes. Your man is making money too, so I don't even know why you're so cheap," Parris replied with a laugh, shaking her head.

"The more money I spend on food, the less money I'll have to spend on these shoes, panties, and purses that I love to wear. See …," said Michelle, holding up her purse.

"Look at your spoiled ass," Parris replied.

"And … You trying to act like your man don't be spoiling your ass either. You know he's making plenty of money over there at that law office," said Michelle.

"Yes, he is, but I would rather see him more than I would want to spend money. Now, tell me; how often do you get to see your man?" Parris asked.

"You mean like a whole day or just when I can?" Michelle asked.

"My point, exactly. If you had to ask me that, then you barely see him. I can't say anything because I barely see Brendan either. But he needs to give me more time. He has been acting funny lately too," said Parris

"What do you mean?" Michelle asked.

Not Settling for Less

"Well, he is always coming home at odd hours of the night," Parris replied.

"Well, what does he say about it?" Michelle asked.

"He just says that he had paperwork to do, or his boss asked him to take care of something for him," Parris replied.

"Well, you know he has to work; it's not like he can tell his boss no," Michelle replied.

"I know, but he has also been getting home and locking himself up in that office and texting on his phone all times of the night. When I do ask him, he says it's his boss. So, I just don't say anything because I don't want him to think I don't trust him," Parris replied.

"Well, do you?" Michelle asked.

"Well ... Ya, I guess ... Just hope that he's not doing anything behind my back," Parris replied, looking somewhat down.

"I'm pretty sure he's not. He seems like a good dude. You didn't marry him for no reason; I'm sure. That was a day that I've seen you the happiest than I've ever seen you in a long time," said Michelle.

Chapter 3

"Ya, you're right. I'm pretty sure it's nothing. I guess I'm just aggravated because I'm not seeing him like I would like to," Parris replied.

"Besides, he's the one who has you living in that big ole house; you and that sexy man of yours," said Michelle.

"Don't push it now. I know my man is fine, but that's my business," Parris replied.

"Girl don't nobody want your man. I got my own sexy chocolate man. Mmm mm mmmm ...," said Michelle, shaking her head.

"You're a mess," said Parris.

"I know, and ... So, what's your point?" Michelle asked with a smirk.

"Girl, what am I going to do with you?" Parris asked.

"Love me. Nothing more, nothing less," Michelle replied with a smile.

They finished their meals and went their separate ways because their schedules clashed from that moment forward.

A little later, Parris finally got home from a long day at work, dropping her purse at the door and heading straight to

Not Settling for Less

the kitchen to take something out for dinner. Her feet were killing her as if they had been run over by a Mac truck. She opened the freezer, looking at and moving things around. "Humm, I'm going to make a pot roast for my baby tonight, with some mac and cheese, with corn on the cob," Parris said with a big smile on her face.

Pulling the meatloaf out of the freezer, Parris placed it in the sink, turning the water on low so it could start defrosting while she settled in. She walked back into her room and grabbed some shorts and a shirt. Then she eased off into the bathroom and cut on the shower. Stripping off her clothes, she wrapped a towel around herself. She then took her clothes into the closet and tossed them on the pile of clothes that had grown tremendously tall. The moment the clothes left her hand, time seemed to slow down as they floated through the air. As the clothes twirled in the air, the condom wrapper from the night before sparkled as the closet light hit it. Parris noticed a twinkle, but she was so ready to hit the shower that she told herself that she would check it before washing the clothes later. FLOP! The clothes finally hit the pile as she walked off.

Chapter 3

"All those clothes! Looks like I'll be washing clothes while I cook," Parris said as she went into the bathroom, closing the door behind her.

While over at the office, Brendan was at his desk, doing some work, when Janae walked in and closed the door behind her.

"Yes, how may I help you, Janae," Brendan asked, looking up at her. He then fixed his eyes on his desk and continued working.

"Just stopping by to see you. Haven't heard from you since lunch. It's going on 6:00 p.m.," Janae replied.

"Well, you know I have work to do and don't be calling me boo at work. This is my job. What we do outside of work stays outside work," said Brendan.

Trying to brush off what Brendan just said, Janae walked up behind him at his desk and tried to rub her hand across his shoulders. Before she could say anything, he grabbed her hand and stood up, getting in her face.

"Bitch! Didn't you just hear what I said? If you keep on with this, you're going to make me ...," Brendan said, grabbing her hair roughly.

Not Settling for Less

Janae snatched her head back and slapped Brendan in the face.

"You better watch your mouth, young man, before I have to punish you," said Janae.

Brendan gave Janae a crazy look. "Damn, girl! I like it when you get feisty," he said as he kissed her, but Janae forced him off her.

"Guess you're going to have to wait till later," Janae said as she walked out of the office, leaving Brendan stuck in his tracks.

Brendan sat down back at his desk. "Man, that girl is going to get me in trouble," he mumbled to himself, straightening his tie.

Back at the house, Parris had just got out of the shower and dried off. "It feels good to finally be clean," she said. Reaching under the counter to get some deodorant, she noticed that she had one more pregnancy test. Wanting to have a family for so long, she decided to just take it. A couple of minutes went by, and she checked the results; the test dared not to let her down this time.

Chapter 3

"Oh, shit!" Parris exclaimed in shock. Jumping around, the excitement drowned out everything else that cluttered her mind. Nothing else mattered. She stood in the mirror, sticking out her stomach. She pretended like she had a pug of a stomach. She placed her hand on the lower parts of her stomach, looking up, smiling. Although she was over ecstatic, she didn't want to tell Brendan yet. She wanted it to be a surprise, even though she doubted that his heart would flicker the same way hers did. It seemed that he didn't want a family at times. While other days he did, his mind changed like Florida weather.

There were so many emotions that clashed with her mood to the point where she didn't know if she wanted to smile or cry. She walked into the room and sat on the bed for a second. Then she jumped up and grabbed her phone. "I got to call my girl," she said. She scrambled through her phone, pushing her finger down to Michelle's name. She waited as the phone rang, so impatient at the time.

"Hello," Michelle answered the phone.

"Hey, girl! You will never guess what happened," said Parris.

Not Settling for Less

"What, girl! You're sounding all extra happy," Michelle quizzed.

"Because I am happy ... I'm ... I'm ... I'm Pregnant. Ahhhh!" Parris screamed with excitement.

"Are you for real, girl? Stop playing ... I can finally be a God mom," said Michelle.

"Yes, you will, girl," Parris replied.

"Is Brendan happy about it?" Michelle asked.

"Well ...," said Parris.

"Girl don't tell me that you haven't told that man yet," said Michelle.

"Well, I just found out a few minutes ago. I'm going to tell him, but I'm afraid he won't agree with it," Parris replied.

"But you still have to tell him, whether he accepts it or not," said Michelle.

"I know, girl. I will; just want it to be special," said Parris.

"I can't wait to go shopping; I finally have someone to spend my money on besides myself," said Michelle.

"Ha! Girl, you're a hot mess," said Parris.

Chapter 3

"Girl, tell me something I don't know. But know that I'm going to be a mess with a handful of baby stuff," Michelle replied.

"Ha-ha! What am I going to do with you?" Parris asked.

"Hopefully nothing; that's why you have a man," Michelle replied, laughing out loud.

"Ugh, your nasty butt," said Parris.

"You're calling me nasty, but who's pregnant again?" Michelle replied.

"Whatever! I'll talk to your nasty self later," said Parris.

"Blah! Ha-ha! All right, girl. Talk to you later," Michelle said with a laugh.

"Bye, girl," said Parris as she hung up the phone. BLEEP! She tossed her phone on the bed and put on something to wear so she could wash up the clothes—which had started to overflow onto the floor like an overfull of glass. Even though she was aware of what awaited her, she walked into the closet and grabbed a handful of clothes, placing them in an additional basket that she had in the laundry room, almost forgetting to prepare dinner. "Oh, let me put on

Not Settling for Less

this food," she said as she dropped the clothes and headed towards the kitchen, burying the poison deeper into the load. Now, it was hiding from the human eye for the time being. So, the wrapper was still consumed by the darkness; it was only a matter of time before it came to light.

Getting to the kitchen, Parris got the roast, put it in a pan, and sprinkled the herbs of choice across the top of the beef that would soon be matured into a feast of all feasts; one that would reach deep down to the bottom pits of hunger and crunch her husband's pains. She also grabbed a pot to start the Mac & Cheese, which had grown to the liking of Brendan's taste buds, and one final pot for the corn on the cob. Now, she was preparing a dinner fit for a king—her king.

Chapter 4

Chapter 4

Uncovered

It was 8:35 p.m., and Brendan was getting ready to leave work when Janae walked in his office. He looked up at her as she closed the door behind her. A cascade of dark shadows surrounded the office like a sin hidden in the deepest crevasses on earth. The outer office had grown dark from the emptiness that had started to spread through the building like a disease. Only a couple of lights kept the floor company. Janae started easing toward Brendan, walking as if she was trying to seduce his soul. His eyes scaled her body like a perfectly painted canvas. Knowing he had a wife at home only sustained his appetite for an eager minute. Eyes red as the devil himself; body growing tired of all these long evenings. While the devil manipulated his mind, his wife was home preparing his dinner, ecstatic from the news that she had acquired earlier that day from the stick of positive possibilities. Parris had forgotten about everything else after

Not Settling for Less

dinner was prepared. She grabbed her iPad and surfed the Internet, looking for baby clothes and toys.

Wanting to give her baby more than she was blessed with when she was younger, Parris typed in stuff, and she noticed that other websites appeared in her web browsing history. "What in the hell! Brendan, really? His nasty butt is all on my iPad looking at porn. Men!" said Parris, looking crazy, distracted from what she had found that she no longer wanted to search. "Oh, damn! I almost forgot that I need to wash these clothes; got to make sure my man is looking good with his nasty self," Parris said as she turned off her iPad, got up, and went into the room.

Parris opened the door and walked over to the closet so that she could grab the clothes and start washing them. She grabbed a handful of clothes once more and began to put them in the basket. The condom wrapper was buried so deep that it was entwined in the clothes. So, once again, the secret that lay deep in the bundle of clothes was far from being uncovered.

A secret capable of causing a heartbreak that would come in more than one shade as well as break in more than

Chapter 4

one place. She picked up the basket and headed to the laundry room. Placing that basket in the laundry room, she went back to grab the other clothes. Coming back to the room with the basket, she sat it on the floor and started to separate the colored from the white, starting with the whites, of which there were very few.

She started un-balling the socks one at a time and turning the shirts inside out. After she had separated the whites from the colors, she cut on the washer and added wash liquid and a little bleach. Grabbing the clothes off the floor, she tossed them into the washer, looking through the rest of the clothes, making sure she didn't leave any whites mixed in the colors. Moving the clothes around, she reached into the other basket and grabbed a couple of colored shirts at once.

The wrapper was balled up in the shirts that she had grabbed. Time is growing slim for secrets to be foretold. Secrets that would crush a delicate heart, a heart that had grown so deep in love over the last 5 years. She tossed the shirts into the load and closed the top, still unaware of what may trigger a painful penetration. She exited the laundry room, cutting out the light and closing the door behind her, as the machine washed the load of laundry.

Back at the office, Brendan and Janae had finished up their extreme activities, sweating like they had just run a marathon. Brendan was laid back in his office chair, and Janae was gathering her clothes. Janae was putting on her clothes while Brendan looked at her, staring at her sexy legs locked in like a prisoner in a jail cell.

"Girl, you are turning me into a sex slave," Brendan said, shaking his head.

"So, now it's my fault that you're a sex machine?" Janae replied.

"Who came in whose office?" Brendan asked.

"Don't act like you didn't want it," Janae replied.

"I plead the fifth," Brendan replied.

"My point, exactly. You know you are feeling me just as much as I am feeling you," Janae said as she tucked her shirt back in and walked over to Brendan. Buttoning up his shirt and straightening his tie, she asked, "Are you good now, Daddy?"

Chapter 4

"I'm as good as a check on Friday," Brendan said with a smile.

"You need help," Janae said with a smile, shaking her head.

"I just had some. But I have to get up and go home. I'll talk to you later," said Brendan.

"Whatever! You need to be coming home to me," Janae replied as she walked towards the door.

"Now, I don't feel like going through this today. You need to have some patience," Brendan replied.

"Patience, really? How long has it been, Brendan?" Janae asked.

Brendan just shook his head.

"Ya, that's my point, exactly. But you can go ahead and enjoy this while you can because no one has a clue of what tomorrow holds," said Janae.

Brendan looked up at Janae as she exited the office. Once she was gone, he got his stuff together and headed out of the office. He walked out through the office door and felt a pair of eyes staring him down. Looking around, he noticed that the new girl Tami was looking at him, smiling like she

Not Settling for Less

knew the secret everyone else seemed to be so blind to as if it was a birth defect.

30 minutes later, Brendan had pulled up to his home, headlight piercing the blinds like the rising of the morning sun. Parris had just finished dinner. She noticed the lights flashing outside; the house was lit up, and it smelled like it was Thanksgiving morning. So anxious to cater to her man, she had forgotten all about the clothes that had come to a tumbling stop in the dryer. Her mind was filled with the deepest sensation of the beginning of a full family—something she had wanted her whole life. She only brought it up a couple of times since it wasn't at the top of Brendan's list of things to do. Brendan wasn't yet at a point in his life where he wanted to be a father. His father was a rolling stone, so he was afraid of not being a good father because he wasn't raised by one himself.

Brendan's mother was a very successful woman, and she taught him everything, but the so-called stage that he was going through, she would be highly disappointed if she knew what lay in his closet of secrets; secrets that any mother would be assumed to have unknown. Brendan got

Chapter 4

out his phone, put it on silent, and placed it in his cell phone holder. He jumped out of the car, grabbed his suitcase, and locked the door behind him. He checked his clothes as he walked toward the front door, making sure nothing looked out of place. He pulled out his keys and unlocked the door. When he entered the house, he was greeted by his wife.

"How was work, honey?" Parris asked with a smile.

"It was OK, honey," Brendan replied, sniffing the air. "It surely smells good in here. Mmmm! Mmm! Mmmmm!" Brendan added.

"I'm just trying to cook a little something for my man," said Parris.

Brendan kissed Parris. "Oh, is that right?" he asked.

"Yes, it is," Parris said with a smile.

"You seem to be in a really good mood tonight. Is everything ok?" Brendan asked.

"Yes, everything is fine; just had a pretty interesting day," Parris replied.

"Oh, OK. So, what was so interesting?" Brendan asked as he walked toward the room.

Not Settling for Less

"I'll tell you in a little, but first, go take a quick shower and get comfortable. I will set the table so we can have a nice dinner together," said Parris.

Brendan walked into the room, got his stuff together, and then jumped into the shower. Parris set the table and lit a few candles. She was so excited about her surprise; all she could do was smile. About 10 minutes later, Parris had the table all set up, and Brendan had just gotten out of the shower.

He walked out of the room with some basketball shorts and a white tee shirt on, pretending to be this innocent man, but he held a fake love that wouldn't bear the test of time. A hurtful destiny for whoever takes in its spiteful means. He smiled at Parris as he took a seat at the table. Parris lit up with excitement, smiling undeniably, happy about what may come as a surprise to him, while scared deep inside that he may not approve.

"You seem a little extra happy today. Did something exciting happen today?" Brendan asked, wanting to know what was on her mind.

Chapter 4

"Well, I guess you could say that" Parris replied as she ate her food.

"Oh, OK. Dang, girl! You put your foot in this," Brendan said as he ate his food like it was his last supper.

"Of course! Got to make sure my king is good. I figured I would make your favorite today," Parris replied with a smile.

"Oh, is that right? So, what do you want?" Brendan asked.

"Huh, what do you mean what do I want?" Parris asked.

"You must want something if you're doing all of this," Brendan replied.

"So, you're saying that I can't do anything for my man without there being no strings attached? Wow! You really know how to mess up a perfect evening," Parris said, shaking her head.

"What? I was just asking a question. You have the candles, and you made my favorite meal. Just thought you wanted something. So, if you don't want anything, what's going on?" Brendan asked.

Not Settling for Less

"You know what? Don't even worry about it. I'm not in the mood anymore. So, just enjoy your food, and we will try this another time," Parris replied.

"You don't have to be like that," Brendan said. He got up, walked over to Parris, and gave her a hug.

"Please don't touch me. Just go eat your food," Parris said with a disgusting look on her face.

"Fine. You're going to want all this later, so I'm not worried. I'll go sit down and enjoy my food for now," Brendan said as he sat back down.

"Please, I don't know who lied to you. I don't know why you think you got it like that," Parris replied with a crazy look on her face.

"You're acting like this now, but we will see how long that lasts," Brendan said, looking at Parris.

"You better enjoy your food because that's the only thing that you'll be enjoying tonight," said Parris.

"We will see," Brendan said, eating his food.

"Yes, we will," Parris replied as she ate her food and looked at Brendan while he made silly faces at her. She just rolled her eyes and shook her head.

Chapter 4

"That's just why I don't like you now; always trying to be cute," said Parris.

"Cute is for puppies, but I love you, too," Brendan replied.

"Whatever," said Parris. She finished up her food, cleaned off her plate, and washed it off in the sink. "I have to go put up the clothes. Even though I don't like you right now. I hope you're enjoying your food," she said as she placed her plate in the sink.

She rolled her eyes at Brendan again before leaving the kitchen. She walked into the laundry room and started pulling the clothes out of the dryer, placing them in a basket. The clothes had picked up a little static from the dryer, so the wrapper was still under wraps for a minute. She closed the door of the dryer, walked into the room, and started taking clothes out one piece at a time and folding them up nicely and neatly.

She had folded 3 shirts, and the next one would break her or make her. She grabbed the shirt, flopped it open, and the condom wrap fell upon the bed like a thief who had been spotted in the depths of the night. Parris looked at it and noticed that it was open, and all she could do was stand

Not Settling for Less

there and look at that golden wrapper that was lounging on her bed. Her stomach dropped as the wrapper stared her right in the face. She didn't want to believe it, but thoughts clouded her mind like bad weather.

Brendan walked into the room as Parris stood there. He walked over to hug her, and before he knew it, she started swinging at him.

"You better get your hands off me," Parris said, looking at Brendan with anger in her eyes.

Brendan jumped back with a look of confusion on his face.

"Have you been cheating on me, Brendan? I think you better think long and hard before you answer me," Parris said, looking at him as if she wished he would try to lie.

Brendan didn't say anything; he just stood there. He noticed the condom wrapper on the bed, and his heart almost stopped. He slipped up after all this time, and he was finally caught. Unable to come up with anything, all he could do was stand there and look pitiful. Parris walked out of the room with tears in her eyes, pushing him, and he fell back onto the wall. He knew she was hurt, so all he did was bite

Chapter 4

his bottom lip. He wanted to chase her, but he didn't know what to say, so he let her go.

"Dammit!" said Brendan, grabbing the wrapper in his hand and crumbling it up.

Chapter 5

Miserable

Brendan woke up the next morning on the couch with a crick in his neck. Not having Parris to wake him up for work, he jumped up, looking at the clock. "Damn! I'm going to be late," he said as he rushed to the room to grab some clothes. Noticing that Parris had already left for the day without saying one word to him on the way out, he got dressed and headed out to work. No coffee or food was waiting for him on the counter, so he grabbed his suitcase and headed out.

Parris was at work, looking like she was going through something. Her employees knew something was wrong, but no one had enough guts to ask her what was wrong. Michelle was the only one who wasn't scared to speak to her, seeing that they had been friends for a while. She walked up to Parris and grabbed her hand.

"Sweetie, come on; let's go talk," said Michelle. She and Parris walked into her office, and they closed the door

Not Settling for Less

behind them. They both sat down. "What's wrong, honey? We just talked about you being pregnant. Was he tripping about the baby?" Michelle asked.

"No, I haven't even told him yet," Parris replied.

"Parris, why not? Well, if that isn't what's wrong, then what's going on with you?" Michelle asked.

"Girl, when I tell you I've never felt so hurt in my life ...," said Parris.

"Huh? What's going on, girl?" Michelle asked, looking confused.

Parris just started crying. Michelle rushed over to comfort her.

"He didn't put his hands on you, did he? Because I keep my knife," said Michelle.

Wiping the tears from her eyes, Parris said, "Girl, he's not that crazy. I ... found an open condom wrapper in our clothes last night, and I asked him, and all he could do was stand there and look dumb," said Parris.

"Are you serious, girl? I would have beaten his ass if I was you," Michelle replied.

"But I'm not your crazy ass. I'm a manager, and I can't let anyone mess up what I have. I've worked too hard to let

Chapter 5

someone ruin everything. Husband or not, I would like to know who he is screwing around with. I think I gave him enough of my life to at least get that much," said Parris.

"I hear you, girl, but he would have still got caught," said Michelle, and they both laughed.

"Girl, I don't know how your man deals with you," Parris replied.

"Well, to tell you the truth, he's not going anywhere, and he knows that. He doesn't do anything crazy because I had him thinking that I was crazy from the start," said Michelle.

"What do you mean thinking? Your ass is crazy," Parris replied.

"I know we're friends but don't think I won't cut you too," Michelle said, laughing loudly.

"I wish you would," said Parris.

"Oh, you think it's a game, huh?" said Michelle as she reached into her purse.

"Don't play with me bitch," Parris said with a laugh.

"Play with it if you want to; you know I'm crazy," replied Michelle.

Not Settling for Less

Meanwhile, back at Brendan's office, Janae was walking back and forth in front of his office, trying to get his attention. He had started feeling bad about what he was doing to his wife and wanted to stop the affair he had going on, but he didn't want to cut her off yet. He felt something way down deep in his stomach and was scared his wife would leave him. He didn't want to completely shut Janae out of the picture because he might need a backup chick. So, he decided to just back off a little until he found out what was going to happen between him and his wife. Janae finally walked into Brendan's office and closed the door.

"So, you're just going to ignore me?" Janae asked.

"I'm not in the mood today. So, please, don't start," Brendan replied.

Looking confused, thinking that she might have done something, Janae asked, "Did I do something wrong?"

"Yes and no! My wife found a condom in our clothes," said Brendan.

Janae stood there for a minute and didn't say a word. She was happy and sad at the same time. Happy that Brendan was a little closer to being hers but sad because she had never seen him like that. A part of her loved it, but her

Chapter 5

heart knew it was wrong. She knew it was wrong, but all that cluttered her mind was all the hot and passionate sex and the greed of wanting him for herself. Deep in her heart, she knew Brendan wouldn't leave his wife willingly, so there had to be a problem or incentive to get him to leave or for her to leave him, and this seemed like it may be one or the other.

Growing frustrated, Brendan asked, "So you don't have anything to say, huh?"

"I really don't know what to say. What did she say?" Janae asked, curious to know the answer.

"She just asked if I was cheating on her," Brendan replied.

"Did you tell her the truth? I thought you would be happy because we can finally be together," said Janae.

"You really think I would just leave my wife?" Brendan asked.

"Well, yes, that's what you said. So, now that you got caught, you want to have a change of heart? I've been giving you all of me, and all you can say now is, do I think you would leave your wife? For the record, you already left your wife when you decided to climb in between these thighs and

Not Settling for Less

make love to me. So, I can't make you do something that you have already done," Janae replied as she crossed her arms and flopped down in the chair in front of Brendan's desk.

Not listening to Janae, Brendan said, "What am I going to do? I can't lose my wife."

"Really? Are you serious? Now you're worried; you have some nerves. All niggas are the same. Y'all want to do dirt and cry later. You get a good woman and don't know what to do with it. I'm a good woman," said Janae.

"Are you seriously listening to yourself? You really think what you're doing is right. You're trying to steal someone else's husband, and you really think I'm supposed to be with you? If you were, don't you think I would have met you first and married you?" Brendan asked.

"You're talking like I'm the only one doing this; you're talking like your shit doesn't stink. We both did it, but the difference between you and me is, I don't have a husband; you jumped in these panties when you knew you had a wife. So, look at yourself before you try to point your fingers at me. But it's all good. Keep crying like a little bitch instead of dealing with the consequence of your actions," Janae replied.

Chapter 5

"Leave," said Brendan.

"What?" Janae asked.

"Leave now!" Brendan said, raising his voice.

"Fine," Janae replied as she walked out of his office.

Janae had been gone a couple of minutes while Brendan sat at his desk, so demented that all he could do was try to hold back his tears. He wanted to call Parris, but he didn't know what to say. So, all he could do was reach for the phone and draw his hand back. "Damn! I messed up," he said. He noticed that he had received an email, so he opened the email, and to his surprise, it was a video of him and Janae having sex in his office. The email didn't have a name; he knew it was the company's email, but he didn't know who had sent it. He automatically assumed Janae was trying to blackmail him. He took a deep breath and headed to Janae's desk, but she wasn't there. It seemed that she had left for the day, so he hurried back to his office and looked for his cell phone so he could send her a text to find out what was going on. He sent her a text but got no response. That only made him grow even more furious; his temperature was boiling

Not Settling for Less

over the top, while his eyes grew wide, and a chill shot down his spinal cord.

30 minutes later, Brendan was in his car, driving home from work. All he could think about was what Janae was up to and what he was going to say when he saw his wife. This was probably one of the most stressful days of his life. He was stuck between the ignored calls from Janae and the miserable feeling that dwelled in the deepest parts of his stomach, and this only forced him to become depressed; he was losing everything through every second that passed. However, he failed to realize that Janae wasn't ignoring him on purpose; she had just put her phone on silent as she didn't want to be bothered or hear any excuses that Brendan would muster up. His wife didn't totally shut him out; she just wanted him to feel her pain. Wrong deeds never go unpunished. Brendan had to feel the pain and realize that what he was doing wasn't right at all. Parris had been through some bad relationships in her past, and the only thing keeping her head up was the fact that she was married, and she believed that he deserved the chance to at least explain himself. Once that has been done, then God would be the only one to keep her from packing her things and leaving.

Chapter 5

Brendan finally pulled up in his driveway; Parris noticed the lights as he pulled up. Brendan sat in the car for a minute to get himself together. He took a deep breath and let it out; he repeated this several times. He stepped one foot out of the car, and his heart pounded hard in his chest like he was about to do a speech in front of millions of people, cameras flashing, and dead silence that caused his thoughts to tumble around in his skull like a load of clothes.

He finally got up enough guts to walk up to the front door. He took out his key, placed it in the lock, and turned it slowly. CLICK! The lock granted him access. As he walked in, he noticed Parris in the kitchen preparing food as usual. She looked up, and he could see the fire burning in her eyes. All he could do was crack a half smile, walk into the room, and start getting ready to take a shower. He placed his bag on the floor beside the bed and started to loosen his tie when his wife walked in, crossed her arms, and leaned back on the wall.

"So, how was your day?" Parris asked.

Not Settling for Less

Not realizing she had walked into the room, Brendan was startled when she spoke, jumping a little as he turned around. "It was OK," he replied in a shaken-up manner.

"Are you OK?" Parris asked, noticing how tense he was. She uncrossed her arms and went and sat at the foot of the bed.

"Yes, I'm fine," Brendan replied, but the look in his eyes told a different story.

"I know you have had all day to think about what you have done to me and our marriage. I have thought long and hard, and I owe you at least a chance to explain. If I didn't give you at least that much, I wouldn't be much of a wife," said Parris.

Brendan stood there, and then he finally glanced into her eyes, unable to come up with anything.

"So, can you explain? At least give me some sort of explanation. So, have you been cheating on me?" Parris asked.

Brendan looked at her as if he was ashamed and didn't know what to do or say to fix his wrongs. Life had prepared him for many things, but this wasn't one of them.

Chapter 5

Tears trickled down her cheeks. "Wow! So, you did cheat on me. Do you want to be with me?" Parris asked, full of anger.

"Yes, I do," Brendan replied.

"Well, why did you cheat on me? I cater to you all the time, making sure you come home to a hot meal every day, even when I don't feel like cooking. Only to find out you didn't even deserve all that. It hurts me to know you would even think about doing something like that to me. I've always been faithful to you, and I've never even thought about stepping out on you. Is it so much to ask for the same from my husband?" Parris asked.

"No, it's not," Brendan replied.

"If it's not, why is it so hard for you to give me that much respect?" Parris asked.

"I know I messed up, and I'm sorry," said Brendan.

"So, is it something I'm not doing right? Is it something that she can give you that I can't?" Parris asked.

"No, you're perfect," said Brendan.

"You say that, but if that was the case, you wouldn't have done this to me, Brendan. Dammit!" said Parris.

Not Settling for Less

Suddenly, Brendan's phone rang; he scrambled through his bag to find it. While he was looking for it, Parris was thinking to herself, *It better not be his little mistress.*

Brendan finally dug his phone out of his bag and noticed it was Janae calling him, but he didn't answer. He just forwarded the call and tried to play it off, but Parris knew.

"So, was that her?" Parris asked.

"Ya!" Brendan mumbled, not wanting to lie.

"OK, Well, call her back and tell her not to call your phone anymore," said Parris.

"Really?" Brendan replied.

"Do you want your marriage or not?" Parris asked.

"Of course, I do," Brendan replied as he picked up the phone and called Janae back.

Janae picked up the phone. "Hello," she said.

"Can you please not call my phone ever again?" Brendan said and then hung up the phone.

"Now, if I ever find out you're messing with another female, we are done for good. The only reason why I'm staying this time is because I'm your wife, and I haven't caught you doing anything before. But don't for one minute

Chapter 5

take my kindness for weakness because I will leave you right where you stand," said Parris.

"I know I messed up, but I will make things right," Brendan replied.

"You will never make things right, but you can start by making them better. You can sleep on the pull-out couch in your office for a week, and if you are getting your stuff together, then you can get back in bed with me," Parris said as she started walking out of the room.

"Huh? This is my house too," Brendan replied.

"I know. That's why I'm not making you leave for that week. Good night," said Parris.

Chapter 6

Chapter 6

Blackmail

Brendan woke up the next morning in his office on his pull-out bed, and his back was aching. The ruggedness of the bed has always done some work on his back. He felt as if he was sleeping on metal poles. He sat up, whipped the coal from his eyes, and stretched with a look of agonizing pain. "I don't know if I can make it a week on this thing," he said as he stood to his feet and stretched once more. So used to his wife waking him up, he realized that he was running late again this morning. He hurried to his room to get ready.

45 minutes later, he made it to work. As he walked in, he saw Janae, and she looked at him, turned her head, and went to her desk. Brendan felt ashamed. A few minutes after he had sat down at his desk, his email went off.

"You've got mail!" the computer prompted.

He opened up the message and noticed that it was unmarked again, and he had no idea who it was from.

Not Settling for Less

Message: *Hello, how are you this morning?*

Brendan: *I'm fine; who is this?*

Response: *That's something you don't need to worry about right now.*

Brendan: *What do you mean? You're messaging me.*

Response: *Yes, I am, but who I am will be revealed in due time.*

Brendan: *OK, and when will that be?*

Response: *Don't worry about that, but let's skip the small talk. You have something I want.*

Brendan: *What could I possibly have that you want?*

Response: *You know exactly what I'm talking about.*

Brendan: *No, I don't. I don't even know who I'm talking to.*

Response: *I want a favor.*

Brendan: *What type of favor?*

Response: *I want you to make love to me.*

Brendan: *Make love to you? Look, I don't know who you are or what you're trying to pull, but this conversation is over.*

Chapter 6

Brendan closed out the email. As soon as he closed out the message, he received another email.

"You got mail," said the computer.

Brendan sat there for a second, and the urge for him to know who it was, was killing him, so he opened the message.

Message: *I tried to play nice. Look out of your office at the monitors hanging throughout the office. It's only going to be a second, so pay attention.*

Brendan looked at the monitor and saw the write-up: *I have the video, and it can be displayed here.* Then the picture switched back to regular programming. Brendan responded to the email: *What the fuck?*

Response: *So, I have your attention now?*

Brendan: *Yes, but I promise this better not be who I think it is.*

Response: *So, you're feisty? I like that. Such a turn-on.*

Brendan: *Why do you want me to make love to you? There are millions of men everywhere.*

Response: *Can I ask you a QUESTION?*

Brendan: *Go ahead.*

Not Settling for Less

Response: *Are you a faithful man?*

Brendan: *I wasn't, but I'm trying to be now. So why can't you find someone else to try and blackmail?*

Response: *Because I love the way you pulled her hair and smacked that ass. But the best part was when you got it while she was pinned on the wall.*

Brendan: *What will it take to make all this go away?*

Response: *I already told you. I want you to make love to me. My rules; my time; and last but not least, my way.*

Brendan: *I have a wife. I can't be gone anytime.*

Response: *I have faith in you. I know you're good at what you do. Just be looking for my message. First, I will send you the time; then I will send you the day; then, finally, I will send you the address of the place, and don't be late or try anything because I will have the whole office watching your dirty laundry, and you will lose your job.*

Brendan: *All right. Fine.*

Response: *Great! Talk to you soon.* ☺

Brendan closed out his email and leaned back in his chair. "Dammit!! This is some bullshit," he said.

Chapter 6

Meanwhile, Parris was in her office, talking to Michelle. Things still felt a little crazy for her, but she was dealing with it the best way she could, sitting down in her chair, and eating some grapes. "Do you know that while Brendan I and were talking about that chick he's been messing with, she had the nerve to call?" she said.

"What!! Are serious, girl?" Michelle replied.

"Ya, you should have seen his face. He was looking like a scared little puppy dog," said Parris.

"Haa-ha! I know he was looking crazy. He probably thought you were going to jump on his behind," Michelle said with a laugh.

"Yes, he did. I looked at him, and I know he saw how furious I was. He was shaking after," Parris said, laughing loudly.

"Girl, you are crazy. So, do you think he will do right now?" Michelle asked.

"To think about it, he was looking pitiful, and I don't think he wants to lose me. I'm not saying none of what he has done is right, but I'm willing to give him a second chance if he's willing to do right," Parris replied.

Not Settling for Less

"Well, I'm going to pray for you guys; hope everything gets better. That couldn't be me, though, because both would be dead," said Michelle.

"I know, girl. I don't know why you think you're a cat woman or something," said Parris.

"Girl, what you mean think? I got my catsuit right in the closet. Play with it if you want to," Michelle replied with a laugh.

"Why do you think that was something that I needed to know? TMI," Parris said, shaking her head.

"Don't try to act like you don't have anything in that closet of yours. I know you do, so you can try that pretend stuff with someone else," Michelle replied.

Parris grabbed a sticky note, crumbled it up, and threw it at Michelle. "Whatever!" she said.

"Ya, I know how you and your man are. You didn't forget what you told me that you and he did last Christmas. Do you need me to recap the whole thing for you? Because you know I'm not scared," said Michelle.

"No!! You're fine. Thanks, though," said Parris.

"Oh, OK," replied Michelle.

Chapter 6

"I really don't like you sometimes," said Parris.

"You don't have to like me, but you will love me," Michelle said with a laugh.

"Chile, go back to work," Parris replied with a smile.

Later that evening, Brendan was in his office, and Janae walked by. Brendan called her, "Janae, can you come here for a second, please?"

Janae stopped and thought to herself if she really wanted to go in, but the way she felt about Brendan in her heart overpowered her mind, so she entered his office. She looked at him with a straight face.

"Can you close the door, please?" Brendan asked.

Janae closed the door and stood by the door.

"Come in and have a seat, please," said Brendan.

Janae started walking to the chair that was in front of Brendan's desk, her hips bumping from left and right like a Congo drum. Brendan's eyes watched ever so carefully as her hips slid down in the chair. He had so much going on in his mind, from his wife to trying to figure out who was trying to cajole him into doing something that he wasn't too fond of. For some reason, the feeling that he had for Janae was coming back to the surface like an apple that was being

Not Settling for Less

bobbed for. He looked into her eyes, and she looked back in his, and they both held their ground.

"So, how are you? I haven't heard much from you," said Brendan.

Janae shot Brendan a furious glance. "You know exactly why you haven't heard from me. So why are you trying to act like you care?" she asked.

"You know I care, but you also knew the situation before you got involved," Brendan replied.

"What was that? How you were planning on leaving your wife, but you never have? Or how about how you told me how much you loved me while we were making love but never can seem to find those words when you're not in between my legs? You made endless promises, and which ones have come to pass? Not a single one, but one thing I can say is, you did say you wouldn't leave your wife recently, and the canvas is painted nice and clear," said Janae.

"I do love you," said Brendan.

"Not as much as you love her," Janae replied.

"She is my wife, so what do you want me to say?" Brendan asked.

Chapter 6

"That you love and want to be with me," Janae replied.

"You know I do," Brendan replied.

"You do but not enough to leave your wife, right?" Janae replied.

"Why are we even still on that? You know that's not going to happen," said Brendan.

"Do you miss me?" Janae asked in a seductive tone.

"Of course, I do, but I'm trying to do right. I made a mistake by messing with you and getting you involved in my marriage. So, I'm trying to make things right, but seems like no matter how hard I try, something tries to cloud my judgment. I must stop this, what we have going on, though," Brendan replied.

"Are you sure that's really what you want to do?" Janae asked as she got up and walked over to close the blinds in Brendan's office. She rocked her hips as she walked over to the blinds.

"What are you doing?" Brendan asked as he watched her hips rock back and forth.

"Just trying to see how sure you are," Janae said as the blinds snapped shut; she started walking back toward

Not Settling for Less

Brendan. She walked over to him, cocked up her skirt, stretched her leg around Brendan's lap, and sat on him.

"What are you doing? Get off me right now," Brendan said as he grabbed Janae by the arms, holding her back as she continued to come closer, trying to kiss him.

"Just stop fighting it, Brendan; you know you want it as bad as I do. I missed you," Janae said and kissed him on his bottom lip.

Brendan tried to fight his urge, but the more and more he tried, the more he got flashbacks of all the lovemaking they shared. All those moments ran through his head like the Kentucky Derby. She kissed him once more, and he gave in like a child trying to hold back tears after skinning his knee. He grabbed her hair, and they started kissing wildly. He was sucked right back into the path that he was trying to escape.

Chapter 7

Chapter 7

The Exchange

It was a nice Saturday morning. The sun was shining through the clouds, and everyone was out, parading down the sidewalk, swinging shopping bags; cars were cruising by, with smiles shining through tinted windows. The breeze swirled through the sky like theme park coasters. A perfect day to get out and enjoy life, Janae was downtown, shopping. She peeped through a couple of windows and shared her presents in a couple of stores. It felt good to be out in the town, enjoying a day outside the office. No paperwork; no customers talking her ear off, and no stressful deadlines. She had nothing but freedom and time.

Janae was walking by a store and noticed that they sold panties, so she walked in to check it out. When she walked in, it was like panties heaven. There were panties from wall to wall. Every color you could imagine; every design you could ask for. It was like being in a candy store, but

Not Settling for Less

instead of candy, there were panties in every shape, fashion, and form. All she could do was stand there for a moment and figure out which way she wanted to walk first. Before she could move, she was greeted.

"Welcome to Gorgeous Gems. How can I help you?" Michelle asked as she greeted Janae with a smile.

"Hello," Janae replied with a smile on her face.

"Hello, how are you today? Is this your first time in Gorgeous Gems?" Michelle asked.

"Yes, I would have to say it is," Janae replied.

"OK. Well, I could give you a tour. Come this way," said Michelle.

"OK, cool," said Janae.

"Was there anything in particular that you were looking for, or are you just looking for something new?" Michelle asked.

"I'm just looking for something new," Janae replied.

Michelle showed Janae around; meanwhile, Parris was back in her office, doing paperwork, not realizing just how much she had to get done. She stood up from her chair and stretched. "Mmmmmm," she moaned. She sat down

Chapter 7

again and continued to work; the day was pretty busy. All of a sudden, the office phone started ringing. She answered, "Gorgeous Gems, this is Parris. How may I help you?"

"You are my Gorgeous Gem. Hey, baby! How are you today?" said Brendan.

"Oh, hey, you; this call was unexpected," Parris replied.

"Yes, I know. I know I have been slacking a little lately, but I'm trying to get it together," said Brendan.

"Oh, OK. It's pretty busy here today. I'm swamped with paperwork. How's your day going?" Parris asked.

"It's going OK; just out, running around here and there," Brendan replied as he looked out through the window of his car, stretched back in his seat.

"Oh, OK; hope you're being good," said Parris.

"Why wouldn't I be?" Brendan asked.

"Do you really want to go there?" Parris asked.

"I'm being good, though. So, how long are you going to be at work today?" Brendan asked.

"Oh, OK; I hope so. The store closes at 6 p.m., but we will see how much work I get done from now until then," Parris replied.

Not Settling for Less

Right before Brendan could reply, his phone beeped.

"Hold on a second, honey; got a call coming in," said Brendan.

"OK," said Parris.

Brendan clicked over. "Hello," he said.

"OK … You will be done in about 15 minutes," said the caller.

"Well, I'm parked down by the coffee shop, so just meet me over there."

"OK, see you soon," the caller replied.

"Bye," said Brendan. He clicked back over. "Sorry about that, honey," he said to Parris.

"So, do I have to pick up something, or are you going to make dinner?" Parris asked.

"You know what? I haven't cooked for you in a while; I think I'll cook something for you. What would you like?" Brendan asked.

"Oh, so you're going to let me choose. You really are trying to get back on my good side, huh? Well, let me think for a second," said Parris.

"OK," said Brendan.

Chapter 7

"OK, I know. Do you mind making that shrimp and lobster pasta you made for me on my birthday?" Parris asked.

"Sure! I said I would make whatever you wanted. So, since you said you should be done at about 6 p.m. today, I'll have it ready by then," said Brendan.

"Sounds good. I wasn't expecting this at all today, but thank you," said Parris.

"You're welcome, honey. Enjoy your day. I'll see you later," said Brendan.

"OK, honey. Bye," Parris said with a smile, hanging up the phone. She needed a breather, so she got up and walked out to the floor to help out. She saw Michelle helping out with a customer, so she walked over and joined in the conversation.

"Hello, Michelle; is everything good?" Parris asked.

"Yes, I'm just helping out a new customer. What was your name again?" Michelle asked.

"Oh, I'm Janae," Janae replied.

"Well, welcome. How is your visit so far?" Parris asked.

Not Settling for Less

"I actually love it. I've always wanted to come in here and check it out, but usually, when I'm down here, I'm rushing because I'm usually doing something else. But I'm glad I had time today to come in here and check out everything. You guys have all kinds of panties," said Janae.

"Yes, we do. We specialize in finding the best and most exotic panty collections that we can find. As you can see, we have all sorts of colors and designs," said Parris.

"Yes, I noticed. You know us women have to keep up with our panties because we have to keep our man's attention," said Janae.

"Trust, I know what you mean because my man loves all the different styles," said Parris.

"Ya, Janae. I get a couple of new pairs every week. When it comes to a man, their attention span is short, so little things like this keep them locked in," said Michelle.

"Girl, tell me about it," said Janae.

"Since it's your first time, and I think you're pretty cool, I'm going to hook you up with a first-timer's discount. But under one condition," said Parris.

"OK. What's that?" Janae asked.

Chapter 7

"You have to make us your new panty store," Parris said with a smile on her face.

"That's it. OK, you have a deal," Janae replied.

"OK. Well, Michelle, take care of her, and Janae, it was nice to meet you," said Parris.

"It was nice to meet you as well, Parris, and thank you so much. You girls are going to be seeing a lot of me," said Janae.

"Hope so," Parris and Michelle replied.

Parris smiled and got ready to walk off when Janae asked, "Parris, can I have your number so I can keep up with the new stuff, and yours also, Michelle?"

Parris turned around. "Sure," she replied, handing Janae a business card.

"See you later, Janae," said Parris as she walked off.

"Bye," Janae replied.

Michelle handed Janae her card also. "Here you go! Are you ready to check out yet?" she asked.

"Yes, I think I need to get up out of here before I overdo it," Janae said with a laugh.

"OK, this way," said Michelle as she led Janae to the counter. Michelle got to the counter. Janae followed and put

Not Settling for Less

her panties on the counter; Michelle rang her up. She scanned all the panties that she had selected. Janae noticed that after she had rung up everything, the total came to $65. Michelle put in the discount, and it dropped to $54.40.

"OK. Your total is $54.40. Cash or credit?" Michelle asked.

"Thank you. I'll be paying credit today," Janae replied as she handed Michelle her credit card.

"You're welcome. Thanks for coming by. So, I hope we will be expecting you within the next couple of weeks," said Michelle as she ran Janae's credit card.

"Oh, girl! Trust me, you will! This is my new spot," Janae replied.

"OK. I'm going to hold you to that," said Michelle.

"Trust I will, and you might hear from me before then. Always look for someone to have a girls' night with. Outside of work, I'm always looking for something to go out and do. Need to go out for a few drinks here and there to get my mind off work," said Janae.

"OK, now you're talking. I guess we will have to make that happen," said Michelle.

Chapter 7

"For sure," said Janae.

Michelle finished checking out Janae and then handed her the bag of merchandise and smiled. "See you later," Michelle said as she waved.

"Bye," Janae replied. She exited the store and looked at all the colors as they flooded her eyes, sparkling in her eyes like Christmas had come early—when, in reality, all that had come early was the beginning of her end. Things had started to connect in a way that she wasn't ready for. Everything has a way of coming to the light, and the panties store was just a key to unlocking the darkest secrets. A light that will not only uncover secrets but will also shine a light on hearts that were once clouded and influenced by despite. In the darkest eye of evil's stronghold, God always has a way of reconstructing or demolishing what he had put together by whatever means necessary. Some come to reality before this time comes, but others let temptations cloud their judgment. One thing that is not supposed to be done, no matter the reason, is coming in between something that God has constructed. There will always be a war between what is right and wrong, so there will always be a lesson, whether it's a lesson that was to be learned or not.

Not Settling for Less

Janae walked out as the door closed behind her like a cell behind a prisoner that had no idea what their life had in store. Janae stopped and looked around for a second. She headed to the coffee shop to grab a cup of coffee. She got to the counter, looking up at the display.

"Let me get a regular coffee, dark, with extra cream and sugar," Janae requested.

"OK, will that be all for you?" the clerk asked.

"Yes, that will be it," Janae responded.

"OK, that will be $2.50," said the clerk.

"OK," Janae said as she handed him her credit card.

The clerk swiped her card and handed it back to her with the receipt after the card was processed. "Here you go; it will be just a minute."

Janae moved over to the pick-up area to wait for her coffee. As she stood in line, the aroma clutched her inter soul with delight. That is the only other thing she had grown addicted to besides Brendan. Janae had finally gotten her coffee and headed out to look for her ride. She looked around and noticed her ride was parked a few cars down. She walked over to the car, which had dark tints on the windows

Chapter 7

so no one could see in. She opened the door and got into the car.

"Hey, baby," said Brendan.

"Hey, sorry it took a minute; I had to get my fix," said Janae.

"I thought I was your fix," Brendan replied.

"You are too, but this one helps me start my day off on track," said Janae.

"So, did you find everything you were looking for?" Brendan asked.

"Yes, I did, and I even found some extra stuff, but you will see all that later. I even met a couple of women that were pretty nice, and I think I might have found some girls to have ladies' night with," said Janae.

"I know how picky you are, and you actually found some women that you would want to hang out with?" Brendan replied.

"Yes, I have," Janae said with a smile on her face.

"OK, that's good," Brendan replied as he drove off.

Chapter 8

Chapter 8

Make-up

Brendan had finally made it home a couple of hours before it was time for Parris to get off. He went to the kitchen and took out something to cook. Then he went to the bedroom and double-checked his clothes to make sure there wasn't anything left behind because that wasn't something he wanted to go through again. Things were finally getting better, and he was trying to keep it that way, despite his little slip-ups and the unknown blackmail that was going on at the office. After he had made sure everything was clear, he jumped into the shower to rid himself of all the temptations that were seeping through his pours like a bad case of the flu.

Brendan cut on the shower. He stripped down and brushed his teeth while the water heated up. The bathroom had started to steam up from the luscious, heated water. The steam covered every inch of the bathroom like trees in the

Not Settling for Less

forest. Brendan got into the shower and stood there as the water cascaded over his shapely muscles—looking like water veins that grasped his shoulders and trickled down his back. He grabbed a rag and soaped it up like a bubbly dish liquid, which foamed up in his rag like Christmas snow. He whipped and scrubbed away his temptations as the soap covered his body like a sheet—one that had covered up all his innermost secrets as the water washed his canvas clean as if he was getting a fresh start. His sins were still there, but the soap had cleansed his skin, getting rid of all the dirt and grudge that had taken hold of him like the shadow of evil.

Brendan cut off the shower, and the last drop whirled down to the bottom of the showerhead and sky-dived to the puddle below. He stepped out onto the bathmat, which was as soft as a sheep's coat that had been rummaged various times. The mate pleasured his feet as he thought, *I need to do something special for my wife*. He thought about going to get flowers; he thought about a candlelight dinner; he also thought about running her water and giving her a full body massage. He thought about lacing the bed with rose petals and putting on some slow music to ease her mind. He had messed up so badly that he even thought about doing

Chapter 8

everything together. He only had about an hour and a half to go grab some things. So, he had to get a move on it. There was a rose truck not too far from him and a dollar store where he could pick up some candles. With enough time wasted, he dried off and hurried to his room, threw some shorts and a tank top on, and headed out, locking his door behind him. He jumped into his car and faded off into the evening glow.

A couple of minutes later, Brendan pulled up to the flower truck which was parked at the gas station across the street from the hospital. He looked and noticed the new girl Tami from the office. She had on a red dress that showed every curb of her body. It was laced with black and silver crinkles. She had on some heels, with red lips all over them. Her hair held soft, luscious curls that fell over the left side of her face. She had a soft shade of red lipstick that made her lips look more welcoming. She was 5'3 and about 120 pounds soaking wet. Looking so tempting, all he could do was stare. She was a breathtaking sight from nothing less than the highest peak of the heavens.

Brendan finally pulled himself together and mustered the strength to get out of the car. He walked up to the flower

Not Settling for Less

truck and started looking around beside her. Brendan tried to play it off as if he didn't see her standing there. Then he looked over at her and threw on his surprised look.

"Do I know you?" Brendan asked.

Tami looked up at Brendan. "Are you talking to me?" she asked as she looked around.

"Yes, you look familiar. Wait, don't you work at my office?" Brendan asked.

"Oh, OK. Yes, I do. Now I know who you are. Brendan, right?" said Tami.

"You know it; the one and only," Brendan said as he held up his arms.

"Oh, is that right?" Tami said with a smile.

"Yep, but why are you up here looking for flowers? Must be surprising your man," said Brendan.

"So, I guess that's your way of trying to find out if I have a man, huh?" Tami asked, looking at Brendan, waiting for a reply.

"No, not really, but why else would you be looking at flowers?" Brendan replied, avoiding what she had asked.

"No, that's not the only reason I might just like flowers, or better yet, I could be buying flowers for my sick friend at the hospital. So, which one do you think it might be?" Tami asked.

"I'll probably go with the sick friend," Brendan said with a smile.

"Good answer. Ya, my friend is sick, so I was coming to get her some flowers and stop by to check on her," said Tami.

"That's nice of you. By the way, you look totally different than you do in the office. Like, wow. Umm ... yeah," said Brendan.

"I'm going to take that as a compliment. Thank you. Excuse me for a second," Tami said, grabbing a bundle of flowers and handing the florist $10.

"Thank you, sir," said Tami.

"Well, don't be a stranger; you can stop by and say hi sometimes," said Brendan.

"OK. Well, I might take you up on that. Enjoy your night. See you later," said Tami.

"Most definitely! You enjoy your night as well. Good night," Brendan said, waving at her as she walked off.

Not Settling for Less

Side-tracked for a minute, Brendan had almost forgotten why he even came to the flower truck. He looked for the flower guy.

"Sir, can I get a dozen roses, please?" Brendan asked.

"That will be 10 dollars," replied the flower guy as he handed Brendan the roses.

Brendan took the flower. "Thanks," he said as he headed back to his car. He got in and drove off.

Brendan made it back home. Looking at his watch, he noticed that he had about an hour before his wife got off work. Brendan grabbed the roses off the front seat and rushed into the house so he could prepare a special night for his wife. His focus was mostly set on Tami; he was trying to get her perfectly constructed body out of his head. A sight that he didn't know existed, based on the work clothes that blemished her true beauty. Walking in through the door, he placed his keys on the countertop. He checked the hallway closet for some candles. Luckily, he found some that he could use that would serve his wishes very nicely.

Brendan had about 10 candles to play with. He placed 5 in various areas in the front room; he placed 1 in the middle of the kitchen table, and the remaining 4 in the

Chapter 8

bedroom (one on each nightstand, and the others on the dresser). He didn't light them, for he didn't want them to burn out. So, he waited. He headed to the kitchen to put the food on. He took out a pot, filled it with water, brought it to a boil, and dropped the Alfredo noodles in boiling aqua. While it was boiling, he placed two lobster tails in the steamer, with some shrimp. He got garlic, seafood seasoning, and garlic powder over the top.

Brendan left the food on and decided to handle the rest of his endeavors. He got two dozen roses and placed two in a vase in the center of the dining room table; he then placed two at the foot of the bed. He peeled the petals off the rest and sprinkled some on the dining room table and the floor around the table. He also sprinkled some on the bed; he then made a trail from the front door to the kitchen table, and from the kitchen table to the bedroom.

Meanwhile, an hour had passed, and back at the store, Parris was just getting off. She locked up the store, jumped into her car, and headed home. About ten minutes later, she pulled up to her house and looked around as she unlocked the door. She opened the door and looked around;

Not Settling for Less

the living room showed and expressed that she had been missed. The mood was dim, and the candle lights soothed the scene like a romantic movie. The rose petals made her feel like a queen, and they were the path to her kingdom. There was soft jazz that massaged her eardrums as it pierced her soul, forming a relaxing sensation that captured all her innermost desires; she felt as if she had been abducted by beings from another planet.

Brendan made Parris feel like she did the first time they met—when he stole an arrow from Cupid that daggered her heart. After her eyes took a breath, the aroma of some succulent shrimp and lobster knocked her sense of smell off the ballpark, smothering her hunger urges like perfect gravy over a tender roast. A meal that was nonetheless fit for a king or, in her case, a queen. All the problems that they were going through just ended up fading out like the end of an R&B classic. Her body had gone from room temperature to X-rated. She followed the rose petals that were ever so gently placed over the floor leading toward the kitchen table. Brendan stepped out of the bedroom in an all-white suit. Parris heard Brendan whisper "Baby"; she turned around and saw him standing there in a tux, holding a rose in his

Chapter 8

hand. He walked up to her and bent on one knee, with his head bowed, as he slowly raised the rose toward her.

"Here you are, my lady; your company has been awaited," said Brendan.

Parris covered her mouth with her hands, as a tear dropped from her eye. "Wow! Brendan, all of this for me?" she asked.

"Of course, my lady," Brendan replied in his British accent as he looked up into her eyes.

Brendan stood to his feet and hugged Parris, caressing her back softly as her hair tickled his nose.

"Let me take your purse; have a seat, my lady," Brendan said to Parris as he pulled out her chair and tucked it under her as she took a seat.

Parris looked at the nicely arranged table as the candlelight danced for her just as kids would around an open fire.

"I have prepared you a wonderful meal this evening," Brendan said as he looked at her as if she was his most prized possession. Parris could feel it; all she could do was smile. She had been blushing since she walked in through

Not Settling for Less

the front door. If an apple was brown, she had surely changed it to red. Brendan had started preparing her plate, and she looked at him as if she wanted to skip dinner and go straight to foreplay. The suit he was wearing made him shine like an angel right out of heaven.

"Look at my baby looking all sexy in that tux," said Parris.

"Just threw on a little something," Brendan replied.

"You did that, boy," Parris said, smiling from ear to ear.

Brendan had finished making her plate and sat it down in front of Parris. "Dinner is served," said Brendan.

"Thank you, baby," Parris said as she looked at the chef-certified meal prepared by no one other than her husband.

They sat down and enjoyed their meal together, laughing and talking about everything that they had forgotten about. Memories never get old, but they can be forgotten if they aren't recapped occasionally. There had been so much time that had passed since they enjoyed each other so much. It was another moment to add to the list. Hopefully,

Chapter 8

their love stands the test of time, for time can enhance or decay a marriage.

After they had finished eating, Brendan walked Parris into the room, where they locked themselves in for the night to share a night of the best lovemaking that they have had in a while—something they both needed, for they knew not what tomorrow would bring.

Chapter 9

Initiation

The next morning, Brendan was just starting to feel like things were getting back on track for him and his wife. Even though things seemed so right at the moment, his feelings weren't just with her; Janae was a common face as well. He knew it wasn't right, but he had fallen too deep and couldn't find a long enough ladder to get him out. His life seemed complicated and overwhelming at times. The sin of lust was just a mere situation that had taken hold of his life, and there was also still an unknown stranger who lurked behind an email.

Brendan got dressed and stepped out through the door; he looked up at the sky that was spray-painted with all the colors of life. A sight that painted a picture in his head, stating that it would be a great day. Well, at least, that's what was imagined—the only way he could try to keep his head off the situations that continued to darken and cloud his judgment. He jumped into his car and headed off to work. Making it to work several minutes later, he got out of his car and walked into his office building as if his night was collaged all over his face. Even Janae could see how he shined from within, which made her soul itch. His attention should only be on her while he was at work, but he walked right past her with a misallied smile that she didn't care much about. She turned and looked at him with spite, for her feelings had grown pit-status.

Brendan finally made it to his desk, and the first thing he did was get his papers out of his suitcase and power up his computer. When his computer had powered up, he logged in and noticed that he had acquired some emails. The first thing he thought about was the unknown person who was trying to blackmail him; his nerves grew tremendously unstable as he proceeded to open his messages. To his amazement, he didn't have any unknown messages. The only thing that was there were a few messages from his boss asking for information about his projects and a couple of messages from some potential clients, which was always good news.

Chapter 9

Janae walked by Brendan's office and gave him a compliment, but he was so happy about his last night's activity that he brushed it off. He opened his messages and got to work. First, he replied to his boss, and then he opened the business emails, called the potential clients, and gave his spill. He had got comfortable because he knew that it wouldn't be easy to reel in these specific clients. These were two of the hardest clients to get; that's why they had become his responsibility. His boss had given him the name 'The Shark,' and the shark killed doubt. In other words, he had to make them feel like that was the place that they needed to be.

A couple of hours had passed, and Brendan had his feet kicked up on his desk as he talked to his new client and twirled a pen in his left hand, so distracted with his conversation that he didn't notice that a new email had just come in. After several minutes had passed, he finally got off the phone, closing the deal with a new client. Brendan jumped out of his chair with excitement, thrusting his arm down to the side like he had hit a home run at the end of the night.

Not Settling for Less

"Yes!!!! Another one bites the dust," said Brendan, sitting back down at his desk in a good mood, ready to get on the next call. As he proceeded to open the email for their contact information, he noticed a familiar email. It was a familiar email that he was eager to see, but one that he despised for numerous reasons. At first, he didn't want to open it; he started sweating like a freshman college basketball player taking the winning shot. All he could do was sit there and look at his computer screen. Finally, he took a deep breath and opened the email. It read:

I know you have been waiting to hear from me since our last brief talk. I was thinking about letting you be, but your tendencies to do the right thing haven't changed. If you're wondering what I mean, just think long and hard about some choices that you have made since the last time I messaged you. My actions reflect your own, but it shows that for everything that is done in life, there is a ripple effect. Even the things that we humans may see as something small; they all play their parts in some shape, fashion, or form. The effect mostly happens to those who don't deserve it, while the committers are free to continue the same path, not caring

Chapter 9

about how it may or may not affect others who are involved in something they mostly don't want to be in and probably don't even have a clue that they are in.

Things seem all fine and dandy until hearts are broken, but does it stop there? Probably not, for those same actions that got you to the place that you're at are the same actions that will keep you in that place. You have people that settle for certain things in life, and you have those who don't put up with it. Then you have those who don't want to put up with it, but they don't know how to get out of it for whatever reason, but enough of that for the moment. I have put together a list of items that I need you to pick up. Then I want you to place them in a safe place until needed:

1. *A small duffle bag*
2. *A sleep mask*
3. *Handcuffs*
4. *Duct tape*
5. *A bottle of champagne*

That will be it for now. So, get all the items that I requested. No need to respond; I will be checking back with you soon.

Not Settling for Less

Brendan looked around, mumbling to himself, "What in the world is going on? This is some crazy shit. A list, really? this is going too far. Man, I don't know what to do. I don't have a choice but to play it out." He sat back on his chair and whipped his hand across his face. After reading that message, his day began to damper down. Growing more paranoid than ever, at first, he thought it was a joke, but reality had finally settled in. A day that twists faith is a day that overpowers minds and causes one to get discouraged, even Brendan, whose heart was made of stone.

Brendan tried to get back to work, but his mind was overwhelmed and anxious at the same time; wanting to know who this secret person was so he could find a way out. He wanted to be clear about this unexpected event. From that moment forward, he would be paying close attention to everyone in the office, for anyone could be behind this reneged activity. *Why would someone blackmail me?* was the question that ran through his head like a stampeding group of gazelles.

Brendan had to get his morale up so he could go tell his boss about the clients that he had finally locked in. So, he

Chapter 9

took a deep breath and put the nonsense to the side; he straightened up his face and walked to his boss's office. As he walked through the office, he strolled at a slow pace and glanced around the office to see if he could notice anything awkward. He approached his boss's office and noticed his boss was on the phone, so he waited outside the office for a minute. While he was standing outside the office, he noticed the new girl, Tami. She smiled and waved, and he smiled and waved back, not realizing that Janae watched as he put up his hand and waved, cheesing with that deceiving smile. Even though it was too late, he eased his hand down slowly as he looked at Janae from the corner of his eye. He turned around, and his boss had just gotten off the phone, so he rushed into his office. His boss looked up as he entered.

"How can I help you son?" Brendan's boss asked.

"I did it again," said Brendan.

"Really? You closed the deal on one of the new potential clients?" his boss asked.

"No, I closed the deal on both of our potential clients," Brendan replied, looking astounded.

Not Settling for Less

"Son don't play. Two of our best tried to close those deals and couldn't, and you're telling me you closed them both?" said his boss.

"That is what I'm saying, boss," Brendan said with a smile on his face.

"That is awesome! You know what? Just for that, you can take the rest of the day paid. That is the best news that I've had in the past months," said his boss.

"Really?" Brendan replied.

"Yes, really. I will see you tomorrow," his boss replied as he stood up and shook Brendan's hand.

"OK, will do. Thanks, sir," Brendan said as he shook his boss's hand back. He exited his boss's office and headed back to his office to shut it down for the day.

Meanwhile, Parris was in her office, doing some paperwork, when she received a text message. The first thing that popped into her head was Brendan, but to her surprise, it wasn't him. It was an unfamiliar number.

"Hey, Parris! This is Janae. I had come in your shop not too long ago, and we exchanged numbers so we could hang out sometimes," Janae texted.

Chapter 9

"Oh, ya! How are you, girl?" Parris responded.

"I'm OK; just at work. I'm having a little man problem," Janae texted.

"I'm sorry to hear that. Do you want to talk about it?" Parris texted.

"It's just a new girl at the office and seems like she's trying to push up on my man," Janae texted.

"Oh, wow! Are you and him having problems, or is it just that?" Parris asked.

"Well, we haven't been seeing eye to eye lately, but he will bounce right back around; he always does," Janae texted.

"Well, I feel you on that because my man has been a headache to me lately. He just got back on my good foot because he was in the doghouse for a while," Parris responded.

"Ya, they need that sometimes. Seems like that's the only way they learn. So, what did you do to get him back in line?" Janae texted.

"Let's just say the couch isn't his best friend, lol," Parris texted.

Not Settling for Less

"Lol. It's not that simple for me. My man doesn't live with me. Sometimes I feel so lost and just want to give it up, but then I fall in love with him all over again," Janae texted.

"Sounds like you really love him; just keep your head up. Everything has a way of working itself out," Parris responded.

"I suppose you're right. What are you up to tomorrow during lunch? Maybe we could do lunch together and chat a bit more," Janae texted.

"That would be nice. Michelle would be with me as well. So, if you don't mind her joining, we could set that up," Parris responded.

"That's cool. I haven't had a girls' lunch in a while; should be fun," Janae texted.

"OK, so we usually take lunch around 1:30. Is that OK with you?" Parris asked.

"Yes, it is," Janae replied.

"OK. See you tomorrow. Ttyl," Parris texted.

"OK, bye," Janae texted.

Brendan got off work and went to the store to find the items on the list. The list seemed like it was from the devil

Chapter 9

himself. The harder he tried to do right; the more difficult things became. Life really has a way of making or breaking someone. Thoughts that continuously clouded Brendan's mind became the least of his worries. After about an hour, he was able to track down every item on his list, and he stored them in an old briefcase in the trunk of his car.

Chapter 10

Lunch with the Girls

The next day, Parris started her day, and just like any other day, she had to open the store, count the registers, and make sure things were looking nice. Getting there before everyone, as usual, she was somewhat excited about lunch with the girls. She had talked to Michelle yesterday and was ready to do a little girl gossip and hopefully find a new friend that she could kick it with. Once the doors opened, the day started, and time started floating by one hour at a time. A couple of new faces and a lot of old ones; paperwork seemed endless, and no matter how hard she worked, she was never able to get ahead until later in the day when things started to slow down a little. She decided that today, she wasn't going to stress over it; she would just take her time and get through it when she could.

Meanwhile, Janae wasn't paying Brendan any attention. She was acting like she didn't see him at all. He

Not Settling for Less

wasn't used to that kind of attention, so it kind of bothered him. When he walked into the office this morning, he smiled at her, but she didn't respond at all. She just continued what she was doing, and he couldn't do anything but look crazy and wonder what was going on. Not only was he dealing with the whole situation with this blackmailer, but he was losing Janae also. Even though he was trying to be faithful to his wife, there was just something about Janae that he couldn't let go of. It might be the control that she has over him, with her take-charge technique that leaves him with his mouth wide open, or the way she looks into his eyes before they start making mad, passionate, hot love. Maybe even the variety of endless panties and bra sets that make her irresistible to him in every way. Whatever it is, he just can't muster the courage to let her go.

Even though Janae was playing like she didn't see Brendan, he was the most noticeable person in the entire office, yet she was trying to break him. She was trying the ignore technique because she wanted to try something after the text conversation that she had with Parris last night. Besides, she knew she would be able to get plenty more ideas and tricks to get what she wanted after lunch with the

Chapter 10

girls. This was something that she had been thinking about most of the night and when she woke up this morning because she couldn't remember the last time, she had a conversation with just girls.

They were supposed to have lunch at about 1:30 p.m., and it was noon at the moment. So, Janae just kept doing her work until that time. She forgot that she didn't ask where the meeting place was, so she took out her phone and texted Parris.

"I know it's not time yet, but I forgot to ask where we are meeting for lunch," Janae texted.

"Oh, I did forget to tell you, huh? Lol. Well, do you know about the restaurant on Kings Ave. called Jenny's?" Parris responded.

"Oh, ya, I know about that restaurant. They have the best mac and cheese," Janae texted.

"Oh, so you do know. Well, we will see you there soon. Ttyl, girl," Parris responded.

"OK, see you soon," Janae texted.

Not Settling for Less

They both got back to work until it was time for them to meet up. Paris started back on her paperwork, and Janae got back on her calls.

Meanwhile, Brendan was trying to figure out what was going on with Janae and what was up with this blackmailer. The way Janae was acting was new, but the blackmailer he had grown tired of. It was like a game that he had no control over, and not having control wasn't something he cared much about. That was the first time that he was forced to deal with a situation that was out of his reach.

He just calmed his nerves and stared back, trying to put his thoughts on his work. He had noticed that most of the morning, he had not heard from the mysterious email manipulator. It was almost 1 p.m., and there wasn't a beep. Not that he was disappointed, but he just wanted this to be over and done with so he could get back to his partially complicated life which he was trying to sort out.

The pressure wasn't doing anything but growing as the day went by, and no progress seemed to slide his way. His luck was like a raindrop that had fallen from a cloud; there was no way to avoid hitting the ground. The situations that had become a part of his life almost seemed like they

Chapter 10

were bound to happen or could be a force of nature where you reap what you sow.

1:30 p.m. finally hit, and the girls got their stuff in order at their offices and were headed for Jenny's. The way Janae had left the office had Brendan wondering where she was headed, for she had never left the office like that in such a hurry. Even though that was not the focus of his worries, it still caught his attention.

Janae had made it to the location. As she started walking to the building, she pulled out her phone and started texting Parris.

"I'm here. Did you guys make it yet?" Janae texted.

A couple of seconds later, a text came through. "Yes, we are inside; just let the host at the front know that you're here with us. I let her know you were on the way," Parris responded.

"OK, cool. Here I come," Janae texted.

Janae talked to the host, and the host led her back to the table. On the way back, she could smell everything. The food smelled so good, and her stomach was locked on like a seeking missile. She hadn't been there in a while, and she

Not Settling for Less

was ready for a nice-sized bowl of homemade Mac and Cheese. She was walking up to the table, and the girls were excited to see her. They both got up, smiling, and hugging her; then they all took a seat.

"Hey, girl! I see you made it," said Parris.

"Yes, I'm here finally. I never thought 1:30 would get here," Janae said, laughing out loud.

"I know what you mean, but it's nice to be out with the girls. I'm used to it; just been me and Parris, but it's always nice to have another woman on the scene for a change," said Michelle.

"Dang! It's like that, Michelle; I'm not enough company for you," Parris responded.

"Now, girl, you know I didn't mean it like that; just the more, the merrier," said Michelle.

"Amen to that," Janae replied.

"Oh, OK. So, both of y'all are on teams, huh?" Parris asked.

Janae and Michelle both laughed

"Anyway, how was your day, Janae?" Parris asked.

Chapter 10

"It was pretty good; just ignored my man all day, and I know it got to him because he kept looking at me every time he got a chance," said Janae.

"That's good; he has to learn one way or another," Parris replied.

"Both of y'all got man problems. Don't know how y'all do it. My man doesn't try anything because he knows I'm a crazy bitch, and I will make his life a living hell," said Michelle.

"So, your man has never messed around on you?" Janae asked.

"Not that I know of. I'm pretty good at keeping his attention. He's a good man, though; so, I trust him, and he trusts me," said Michelle.

"You're lucky. I can't seem to find a man worth keeping or one to appreciate me," Janae replied.

"You will find that man just for you soon; just keep your head up, and he will come," said Parris. "Some men just need a little breaking in, and they will be just fine. We are strong black women, so sometimes we've got to show our man why we are strong black women," Parris added.

Not Settling for Less

"All you girls have to do is stay on your man's ass when he is acting up and cater to him when he's not. It's that simple. If he's being good, then treat him good, and if he's doing bad, put his ass in the doghouse," said Michelle.

"I hear that," said Parris.

"Doghouse," said Janae. "You know it, girl. So, how long have you girls been with your men?" she asked.

"Well, I've been with my man forever. We met each other in college and have been together since then. I guess it was just something about him and that smile that just drove me crazy," said Michelle.

"I've been with my man for going on 7 years. He's a headache at times, but he's a good man. He doesn't seem like he wants kids at times, and I do, but he will have to just accept it one day. Things happen when they are ready, and we just have to adapt," said Parris.

"Hold up! Are you pregnant?" Janae asked as she looked at Parris, and then at Michelle, but neither one said anything. "Wow! Does he know?" Janae asked.

"Well, no because he got put in the doghouse before I got a chance to tell him," said Parris.

Chapter 10

"So, when are you planning on telling him?" Janae asked.

"Still trying to figure that part out. I want to make sure he's done with his mess, and a baby is not on his list right now, so it's going to be a little difficult," Parris replied.

"Well, I hope everything works in your favor. Seems like you really want a baby," said Janae.

"If you only knew. She talks me to death about what she's going to do once she gets her," said Michelle.

"Whatever! Don't try to be cute. You've been all in it too. talking about everything you're going to do, also because this is your first God baby. So, shut up with that nonsense because you want one just as bad as me," Parris replied.

"Whatever. So, you're just going to put my business out like that?" Michelle asked.

"Honey, you will be OK. Besides, we are talking about me, not you. So, it's actually my business," Parris replied.

"Just order some food. You've been doing all this talking, and we haven't ordered yet. I'm hungry," said Michelle.

Not Settling for Less

"I bet you are, with your greedy self. Always eating something. Are you sure you're not pregnant?" Parris asked.

"Oh, you just tried that. Don't try me, bitch," said Michelle.

Janae and Parris busted up laughing.

"Just saying; don't kill the messenger," Parris replied.

"Whatever. Where's the waiter?" Michelle asked.

All the girls laughed as the waiter came back around to their table. They all ordered and kept talking to each other until the food came to the table. About 15 minutes later, the food made it to the table, and they all ate and enjoyed each other's company to the fullest, talking about all kinds of things like they all had been friends forever. Janae enjoyed herself very much, and sisterhood was born, despite the unknown truths that lay in the dark—a truth that would make or break them.

About 30 minutes later, the girls had finished their meals; they left their tips and exited the restaurant. Out in the parking lot, they all said their goodbyes and went their separate ways. A couple of minutes later, each of them had made it back to their jobs and went back to work as if they never left.

Chapter 10

Brendan saw Janae come back to work smiling like something was going on, and he was going to make it his duty to find out just what that something was, hoping another man didn't come in and steal her heart away. As selfish as he was, he wanted to be the only guy, even though he wasn't willing to give her his all, as the only way to do that was to leave his wife, and that wasn't a path that he was willing to take.

Chapter 11

Chapter 11

Then the Games Began

Two days later, on Friday, at 8:00 p.m., Brendan was home with his wife. They had been doing well lately; no arguments, and he hadn't been on the couch since the incident. They were enjoying their dinner together when Brendan's phone went off, but it wasn't from a call or text; it was an email notification. So, he checked it because he thought maybe his boss was trying to get in contact with him about a project that he was working on to improve client ratios for the company. When he made it to his phone, he checked it, and surprisingly, it wasn't him. His heart dropped, but he tried to keep his composure because he didn't want his wife to think anything. So, he sat there, trying to play it off long enough to see what his blackmailer wanted.

Brendan started to read the message: *I gave you enough time to get all the supplies that I asked you to get. So, now, it's time to get started. This message will be quite*

Not Settling for Less

lengthy, so you might want to take a minute to grab something to take notes with. So, he got up. "My boss is on my butt about this project," Brendan said so his wife wouldn't think anything of it. He went and grabbed his little notepad out of his office and sat down so he could take some notes. He started to read again:

OK. So, now that you have something to write with, first of all, I hope you took the time to get everything I asked for because I would hate for that video to get out. I'm really not worried, though, because I know what type of man you are, and that's not something that you would let happen if you had a choice. So, anyway, I know you have been trying to find out who I am, but you will find out in due time. Until then, just stay on my good side, and we won't have any issues. I know you have a life, and I also know you have a job. So being able to get out when I need you shouldn't be a hard task for you at all. First, I'm going to need you to bring a change of clothes, which consists of a white tank top and boxers, with some shorts.

Now, that should be everything that you need between the items I asked you to pick up earlier this week

Chapter 11

and those couple of things that you should have lying around your house. OK, since all the items are taken care of now, it's time to get down to business. I know you're probably home with your wife, but I'm sure you can get out. After you get out, I'm going to need you to go down to the Westfield resort off Martin L. King Blvd. and Hampton Ave. Once you get there, go inside to the front desk and check-in. The room will be in your name, so you can use your card to check in. I figured you would ask for my name at the front desk, so I just used your name instead.

Once you have checked in, go to the room and get changed, and you will find a note with additional information. By the way, you have an hour, nothing more. So, if you're not there, then I guess I will have to turn up the heat, starting at the job; then I will have to give your wife a little gift. See you soon.

Brendan took a few notes, got up, and headed to the room so he could figure out how he could get out of the house without his wife thinking anything suspicious. He didn't want to put everything in a duffle bag, for that would be too noticeable, so he just grabbed his laptop bag folded his couple pieces of clothing and placed them neatly inside

Not Settling for Less

so once he walked out, it just looked as if he was carrying his laptop bag. After he took care of that, he found something to wear. With everything ready, he walked out of the room. Looking at his wife, who had finished eating and started to wash dishes, Brendan said, "Honey, I must go out and grab a few things for this project at work. My boss sent me an email with some additional things he wanted me to put together."

The things he would pick up while he was out, were things he had to get anyway; he just didn't have time to get them, so he was going to pick them up after he took care of his business.

Parris looked up. "Honey, you have to go now? It can't wait until tomorrow?" she asked.

"Not really, honey. I'm going to be up a little late tonight, trying to get some work done," replied Brendan.

"OK, honey. Well, are you at least going to finish your food?" Parris asked.

"Can you wrap it up and put it in the refrigerator for me, and I'll get it when I get back?" Brendan asked.

Chapter 11

"Sure, honey. Be careful out there, please, and why are you taking your laptop?" Parris asked.

"Well, I grabbed it just in case I need to take any notes or look over some of my research," Brendan replied.

"Oh, OK, honey. Well, handle your business. I'll see you in the morning. I love you," said Parris.

"I love you too, honey," said Brendan as he walked out through the door and jumped in the car. He took a breath as he shook his head. "This is crazy," he said. He pulled out his phone and found the address to the hotel; he put it in his GPS. Cranking up his car, he started to follow his GPS to the location. He looked out the window as the streetlights grazed off his driver's window.

Brendan was more nervous than a cow getting lured into a slaughterhouse. He hoped that after tonight, all the shenanigans would be over. The closer he got to the location, the more homeless people he saw, and he hoped that this would never come to pass in his life. A man who was so smart had no sense when it came to his relationship and steering clear of problems. One would think wisdom came with age, but the wisdom must have skipped him.

Not Settling for Less

After driving for a little over 20 minutes, Brendan arrived at the hotel. He found a parking spot, got out of the car, grabbed everything, and walked into the building.

As Brendan walked up to the counter, he was greeted by the hotel clerk, "Good evening, sir. Welcome to the Westfield resort. How may I help you?"

"Yes, I have reservations," Brendan replied as he looked around the room for any familiar faces.

"OK. Well, can I get your ID and credit card to put on file for incidentals?" the clerk asked.

"OK. Just a second," said Brendan, looking into his wallet for his credit card and ID. He pulled them out of his wallet and handed them to the clerk. "Here you are, sir," said Brendan.

"Thank you, sir; give me just a second. By the way, how many keys would you like? Never mind; there is a note on the account already," said the clerk.

Curious, Brendan asked, "Well, who placed a note on the account?"

"Well, you did, sir," the clerk replied.

Chapter 11

"OK. Sorry, it must have slipped my mind," said Brendan.

"No problem. Well, we have free Wi-Fi. Just enter the code on the back of your card sleeve. Free breakfast from 6:30 a.m. till 10:00 a.m. If anything isn't to your liking, just give me a call from the phone in your room, and I will take care of you. Thank you, and I hope you enjoy your stay. Goodnight," said the clerk as he handed Brendan his room key.

"Thank you. So, where is the elevator?" Brendan asked.

"It's down the hall—to the left," the clerk replied.

"Thank you, sir," Brendan said, walking off, still looking around.

"You're welcome," the clerk replied.

The tension grew greater the closer Brendan got to his room. He was unsuccessful in finding his potential blackmailer. He finally got to his floor. He looked up at the room number sign, and the arrow pointed to the right. He looked at his card again, Room Number 309, which seemed to be at the end of the hall. He walked up to his door, pulled his card out, opened the door, and walked in with caution.

Not Settling for Less

He looked behind the door, making sure the coast was clear so he could enter. Things were clear, so he walked in and placed his stuff down on the bed quietly. He started to tip-toe around the room, checking to see if anyone was in the room. Now convinced that there was no one in the room, he sat at the edge of the bed and looked around; he noticed a piece of paper folded up on the chair. He picked up the note and began to read:

I see you have made it, but there are a couple of things that I need you to do first. First, I'm going to need you to go take a shower and put on your tank top, boxers, and shorts. Once you have completed that, pull all the items out of the bag and place them on the bed. There should be a couple of glasses by the sink, so you can pour a little champagne into each glass. After that, place the blindfold over your face; then put the handcuffs on, behind your back, but before you handcuff yourself to the chair, place the key on the table, by the TV. I know you're wondering how I will know; just trust and believe that I will. Also, just to give you a heads-up, if you try anything sneaky, your video is on a timer. So, if I'm not back to stop it at a certain time, it will go viral."

Chapter 11

"This is some bullshit!" Brendan shouted. No matter how hard he was thinking, he couldn't find a way out of this situation. So, after sitting down on the bed for a couple of minutes, he just did what he was told. Before he did so, he took a sip of champagne; then he placed the key on the table and took a shower. Then he sat in the chair, placed the blindfold on, and handcuffed himself to the chair. After a minute or two, he started feeling lightheaded. As he shook his head, his eyes grew heavy, and without control, he was out.

After about 30 minutes, Brendan started to come to; his eyes were still heavy, and his vision was blurry. His head was heavy, but he forced himself to look around the room. He noticed someone sitting on the bed in front of him, but his vision was so hazy that he couldn't make out who it was. He was so weak that he couldn't keep his eyes open. Every time he opened his eyes, the shadow of a person grew closer and closer. The closer they got, the more he could make up some kind of body shape. He noticed that they were not built like a guy, so that was a partial relief.

Not Settling for Less

Now that he had that part figured out, he tried to talk, but nothing he was trying to mutter made any sense.

The mistress walked up to Brendan and placed her finger on his mouth. "There is no need to try to speak because you won't be able to for the next 10 minutes or so. So, just relax, and I will take care of you until then. I had to knock you out just to make sure you wouldn't try anything. I have to say you have dealt with everything quite well. I know you're wondering why you. That's all quite simple; your actions and the way you live life pulled me toward you. I like guys who live life and are not scared of who they may hurt in the process. I was once one of those women who cried every time something happened. It took one man to change all of that for me. Now, I'm the one who runs the show, as you can see. No more crying night after night over something I couldn't change. I figured that I may not be able to change stuff that ruined my life, but I can live my life to the fullest and not care who gets hurt in the process. All I know is, my heart will never hurt anymore. I would just like to introduce you to my world. A world where there are no limits. A world where you can be free while you have a chance to. A world where

Chapter 11

there aren't many of us; some of us embrace it, while others feel like they are all alone. But enough talking; let's get down to business," said the mistress.

Unable to fight or say anything, Brendan just sat there and listened. He continued to look, but after a while, he noticed that she wore a mask. Her voice sounded somewhat familiar, but he couldn't make it out. She stripped his shorts and boxers off and started giving him head; he couldn't speak, but he could feel everything. His body screamed inside; he was witnessing some of the best head he had ever gotten. After a couple of up-and-down movements, he cared not to fight anymore. His lustful condition took over, and he was enjoying every minute. Once it starts, there's no going back.

Brendan could hear a voice in his head telling him it wasn't right, but at that point, it didn't matter because he couldn't stop it, anyway, so he just enjoyed it. If he could stop it, after witnessing what he had just witnessed, he probably wouldn't have stopped it anyway. She grabbed a condom and grabbed him sternly on his manhood; she rolled the condom down to the base of his magic stick, which was at full fledge.

Not Settling for Less

She pulled off her panties, for that's all she had on, anyway. From that moment, she graced his presence as she lingered at the edge of the bed, waiting for him to wake up. She slid her leg over him and eased down on it. He was blessed enough, as he forced a moan from her innermost soul.

"Oh my God! Oh yes! Ahhhhhh!" she moaned, riding him, as he sat strapped to the chair. Thrusting her pelvic area on him strongly as she slid up and down, her back muscles tightened as her butt slid on his thighs. "Oooooo, yesss!" she moaned. The more she got into it, the more Brendan was feeling it also.

Brendan's voice was aging by the minute until he was able to force a moan out himself. "Uhhhhhh ... shit!" he moaned.

"You like it, daddy?" the mistress asked.

"Yes! Ooooo!" Brendan replied.

"Would you like to try something?" the mistress asked.

"Sure," Brendan replied.

Chapter 11

"OK, I'm going to take off the condom because I would like to feel all of you. Don't worry; I won't get pregnant. Do you trust me?" the mistress asked.

"I don't know," Brendan replied.

She kissed him and rose up enough so she could slide the condom off, and then she slid back down on it and started riding and moaning as the sounds echoed around the room like an empty stadium. She took control of him for the rest of the night as the darkness consumed the room.

Chapter 12

Chapter 12

A Long Morning

That next morning, Brendan woke up from a deep sleep with a headache. He slowly opened his eyes, looking around the hotel room; his mistress was nowhere to be found. He had handcuffs on one of his wrists, with no shirt, one sock, and the sheet swayed across his skin as he eased up from the bed. He knew he had some explaining to do when he got home.

The sun would beat him home; the clock stared down at him like a homeless person waiting for change. All he could do was shake his head and get up slowly, for the aftereffects of the drugs were wearing off at a slow pace like a bad hangover. He lingered around the room, gathering all his belongings. Still unable to define who his blackmailer was, her sexual urges had been satisfied that night, but a face had still not been matched to his situation. He wanted all this to be done and over with, but the way she seduced

Not Settling for Less

him had his mind wide open, and he was becoming addicted to her. A fix that he couldn't find that hate for, which he thought he was ready to unload on his blackmailer like a magnum clip. The more he tried to hate her, the more he lusted over her, whoever she may be. He finally got over it and jumped in the shower to wash up before he headed home.

He couldn't chance his wife smelling an unfamiliar scent on him. So, he took a quick bath and put back on his clothes and straightened his tie as he jazzed up himself in the mirror. He placed all his items back in his laptop bag and took the room key down to the front desk to check out. He walked up to the desk and handed the desk clerk the key.

"Here you are, sir," said Brendan.

The clerk looked up at him and noticed the room number. He shook his head and said with a smile, "Did you enjoy your stay here at Westfield Resort?"

Brendan shot the clerk a weird look. "Yes, I did. Thank you," he replied.

"OK. You're all taken care of. Enjoy your day, sir," said the clerk.

"Will do. Thank you," said Brendan.

Chapter 12

Brendan left the resort and headed home. Parris had to work this morning, so he had little time to come up with a good reason for not making it back home. He was trying to avoid being in the doghouse again; he didn't want to sleep on the couch again. Even though he didn't feel like this situation was his fault, he didn't know how to tell his wife that he was being blackmailed. Even if he did know how to tell her, it might not be a good idea, seeing that he just technically cheated on her. These were some still waters he was treading. On his way home in the car, he checked his phone, and he had missed calls from his wife as well as text messages. Reading through some of the messages, he could tell his wife was pissed, and he was going to get the business when she saw him again.

Brendan responded to one of the messages, "Honey, sorry I missed your call and messages. I was a little tired, so I ended up pulling into a hotel parking lot, and I was trying to take a little nap, but I ended up sleeping longer than I expected. I guess I was tired. I know you were worried, but I am fine, honey. I Love You." He waited for a response as he continued to drive, but he got nothing. He almost forgot that

Not Settling for Less

he had to grab a couple of things for his project for work. He decided to get what he needed and head home so he could finish up his project for work because his boss wanted it by the end of the day. He had a slight headache, but it needed to be done, and he wasn't going to let something as small as a headache slow him down.

About an hour later, Brendan pulled up in his driveway; he got all his things out of the car and went to his office to get to work. Before he started, he remembered he had his food from last night in the refrigerator; he was starving, and that plate sounded really good at the moment. He heated his food, went to his office, and got to work.

Parris was at work, handling business as usual. Her day was busy; it seemed like everyone was trying to pick up something extra for the weekend. Some women wanted something new because they were hitting the club; some were homebodies and just wanted to surprise their man with a little something extra; some were trying to lock a new man down with tantalizing curbs and good loving. One thing about her job was that she heard all kinds of reasons why women bought panties and bras. Some women were so desperate, while others were taking care of the home, for they had to

Chapter 12

keep their man locked in on them, and nobody else. Parris believed that a man's attention grows short if you don't keep them physically and mentally attracted to you. She also believed that if they aren't acting right, then they don't deserve anything. Nothing kills a man more than his woman not paying him any attention.

Michelle noticed that Parris wasn't in her usual mood; she looked a little down today, and she wanted to find out why and how she could make her feel better. Michelle walked up to Parris. "Can I talk to you for a minute?" she asked.

"Sure! Come on; let's step in my office," said Parris. The girls walked into her office, and they took a seat. Parris was trying to hold her feelings in, but Michelle had been her friend for so long that she could tell when she was keeping secrets. Besides, Parris could not hide her feelings very well, anyway. Parris looked at Michelle and looked down at her desk like she was looking at some paperwork.

"What's wrong, girl?" Michelle asked.

"Nothing, girl; I'm fine," Parris replied.

Not Settling for Less

"Come on, Parris; you know I know you better than that. What's going on?" Michelle asked.

"OK, fine. I'm mad at Brendan again," said Parris.

"What did he do now?" Michelle asked.

"I'm trying not to think negatively, but I'm hoping he wasn't out with that girl again," said Parris.

"What you mean? Wasn't he home with you?" Michelle asked.

"Yes, he was, but then he got an email and said his boss has a project that he needed to be done by today, and he had to go out and pick up some stuff for the project," said Parris.

"Well, maybe he did go out and pick up some stuff," said Michelle.

"The only thing that's bothering me is, he didn't come back home last night. He sent me a text this morning, saying that he fell asleep in his car. I'm trying to believe him, but I don't want to look like a fool again," said Parris.

"I don't know, girl. Just put him in the doghouse for now, and when he gets tired, he will tell you the truth if he did do something," said Michelle.

Chapter 12

"Well, I guess I can do that and see what happens, but how will I know if he's telling the truth when he does try to tell me?" Parris asked.

"Well, you won't, but once he comes to you the first time, ignore him and still make him sleep on the couch, and after a couple of days, he will come to you again, and if his story changes or not, then you will know if he was telling the truth. Then you can choose to trust what he's saying or not, but I think after the second time, he will tell you the truth," said Michelle.

"OK. Thanks, Michelle. You always know how to make me feel better," said Parris.

"Just make sure you stay strong. Find stuff to do until it's all said and done," said Michelle.

"I will. Trust and believe I have plenty that I could be doing. I think I might text Janae and see what she is doing tomorrow and see if she wants to hang out a little. I haven't had a girls' day out in a while," said Parris.

"Sounds like a plan. When I get away from my man, I will hang out with you too," said Michelle.

Not Settling for Less

"OK, thanks. I don't know what I would do sometimes without you," said Parris.

"You know I love you, girl, and I always have your back," said Michelle.

"I love you too, girl," Parris replied.

"So, have you told Brendan about you being pregnant yet?" Michelle asked.

"Um, no, not yet. I've been trying to, but every time I want to, something comes up, and I don't get a chance to," Parris replied.

"Well, you need to tell that man. You can't keep information like that away from him," said Michelle.

"I know. After I find out where he was last night, then I will tell him, "said Parris.

"OK. Well, I'm going to get back to work now," said Michelle.

"OK. I'll be out soon," Parris replied. Michelle got up and walked out of her office; she headed back to the floor. Parris pulled out her phone and started texting Janae, "Hey, girl! I was trying to find out if you were free anytime tomorrow."

Chapter 12

Janae was relaxing on the couch when a text came through. She picked up and replied, "Hey, I'm not doing anything. Why? What's up?"

"I wanted to hang out, maybe do some shopping and lunch. Are you down?" Parris texted.

"Sure, sounds fun. Not talking to my man right now, so I need to get out and do something," Janae texted.

"I guess that makes two of us because I'm not talking to mine either, lol," Parris texted.

"Wow! Some luck we are having, lol," Janae texted.

"Ya, but it's cool because we are going to go out and enjoy ourselves with or without them," Parris texted.

"I hear that. So what time are you talking about?" Janae texted.

"Well, is 10:00 a.m. OK?" Parris texted.

"Sure, that's fine with me. I almost thought you were going to say 8 or something. I would have been like maybe next time, lol. I hate getting up early," Janae texted.

"I'm not a morning person either unless it's work, or I don't have a choice," Parris texted.

Not Settling for Less

"I hear that, but when you get a minute, can you text me your address, and I'll call you in the morning when I'm on my way?" Janae texted.

"OK, I will do it soon; I'll send it to you later. I need to finish up for the day. Talk to you later," Parris texted.

"OK, later," Janae texted.

Parris got back to work to make sure everything was on track so that when the day was over, she could just wrap up and leave. She couldn't help but wonder if Brendan was telling the truth or not. The anxiety was killing her and was almost interfering with her work.

Four hours later, back at the house, Brendan was finishing up his project for work, and it was about time for Parris to get off work. He knew she was upset because she didn't respond to him all day. No matter how much he wanted to keep texting her, he didn't because he still had work to do, and his job was very important to him. He was making progress in the company, and soon, he would be eligible for a promotion and be able to have that long-awaited pay increase. He made the last finishing touches to the project and sent it to his boss. After he had finished it, he got up and started cleaning up the house a little. He was

Chapter 12

already in trouble, so he was hoping that if he cleaned a little, it would lighten the load a little. He probably would be in the doghouse again, so he just had to man up and accept it.

About an hour later, Parris walked into the house and looked around, noticing that the house was clean. She went into the room, and Brendan was in the shower. She didn't speak; she just took a pillow and blanket and put them on the couch for Brendan because that's where he would be for a couple of days. Then she went into the kitchen; Brendan had cooked a little something. So, she made a plate, sat down, and ate. 10 minutes or so later, Brendan came out of the room, ready for bed; Parris looked up at him and continued eating. He walked over and fixed his plate as well and sat down to eat. He looked up and noticed that she wasn't smiling or anything.

"Baby ... Um, I finished my project for work," said Brendan.

"That's good," Parris replied.

"I also cleaned up a little and made something to eat so you wouldn't have to," said Brendan.

"OK, thanks," Parris replied.

Not Settling for Less

"I know you're mad at me, but I really did fall asleep in the car," said Brendan.

"OK, I hear you," said Parris.

"How was your day?" Brendan asked.

"It was good, but I'm not really in the mood to talk, but when you're ready to tell me the truth, let me know. I put your pillow and blanket on the couch. Also, tomorrow, I'm hanging out with my new friend that I met at my store; we are going to have a girls' day out," Parris replied. She finished up her food, got up, and walked into the room, closing the door behind her.

Chapter 13

Chapter 13

Home Visit

It was Sunday morning. Brendan was tucked up on the couch, and as usual, his back was hurting like he had worked all night lifting 50-pound boxes. That was something he hated more than his wife being mad at him. Even though his problems seemed like they wouldn't vanish, he couldn't seem to extinguish them, so he still pushed forward through the smog of life, which started to bully his guilt. The deeper he fell into the pits of life, the harder it would be to get out. It almost seemed like his life was on a course that he couldn't alter, stuck in the middle of the most severe case of adultery that he had created. A life that was made just for him and his wife that he was supposed to be sharing for all the days that God has given him under the sun through all his meaningless days. Coming in between something that was ordained by God is like skating on thin ice.

Not settling for Less

Brendan finally shook it off and sat up; he whipped his face and stretched. His body roared from the agony of the pain that shot up and down his back like a drag racer on a track. He slowly opened his eyes like a baby who had just been brought into this world. He looked at the time; it was 8:30 a.m., and he had a few things that he needed to take care of this morning. He knew Parris was still mad at him, and she was going to be gone most of the day. So, he was going to see if he could find a couple of odds and ends. He got up and walked into the room; he noticed that Parris was up, walking around, getting stuff together so she could head out.

"Good morning," Brendan said as he walked into the room.

"Good morning," Parris replied. She continued to go about what she was doing, getting her clothes together and the shoes that she was about to wear. So, Brendan turned to head out of the room to make some breakfast.

"Would you like me to make you something for breakfast?" Brendan asked.

"No, I'm fine. I will grab something while I'm out." Parris replied.

Chapter 13

"OK," Brendan said as he exited the room.

Brendan walked into the kitchen and put on some grits; then he put some sausage in the oven. He took out a skillet, placed it on the stove, oiled down the pan with butter, and cooked a couple of pieces of toast. He went to the living room and switched on the stereo so he could groove a little while he prepared something for breakfast. 10 minutes later, the grits were almost done, and he could smell the rising aroma of the sausage growing stronger by the minute. He scrambled up a couple of eggs and sprinkled a little cheese across the top.

Meanwhile, Parris had sent Janae a text with her address so she could make it there by 10 a.m. It was about 9 a.m., and she knew Janae was about 20 minutes away, so an hour was plenty of time for her to finish getting ready before Janae made it to the house. A couple of minutes went by, and she received a response from Janae. "OK, I will text you when I'm on my way."

"OK. See you soon, girl," Parris texted.

It was about 20 minutes after 9, and Brendan had finished cooking; he made his plate and then sat down to eat.

Not settling for Less

He sniffed his food and said a prayer in his head. "Amen," he muttered. He looked at his food and said, "Oh yea!" He started eating.

Parris had finished getting dressed. She walked out to the living room about 15 minutes later. Brendan looked up; he was as astonished as usual.

"You look nice," said Brendan.

"Thank you," Parris replied and slightly smiled, even though she was still mad at him.

Brendan saw that Parris had smiled, and it made him feel a little better because yesterday she wasn't smiling at all. He had just finished eating. He got up, washed his plate, and then went back to the room to find something to wear before jumping into the shower. He eventually found something nice to wear just so he could go and take care of a couple of things. He laid his clothes out on the bed, went to the bathroom, and cut on the shower so that the water could start heating up.

A couple of minutes later, the steam was illuminating under the bathroom door like a scene from a horror film. Brendan went into the bathroom, stripped down, and got into the shower. He just stood there for a while, letting the water

Chapter 13

run down his back. It was a tantalizing feeling that he lusted over for a while. That was the closest that he could get to a massaging sensation at the moment because Parris didn't want to be around him any time soon.

Meanwhile, Janae had made it to the house. She rang the doorbell. Parris let her in. "Hey, girl; you made it," said Parris, giving Janae a hug.

"Hey, girl; you ready?" Janae asked.

"Yes, I am but come in for a second. I wanted you to meet my baby," said Parris.

"OK," Janae replied as she came in and took a seat.

"Baby! Baby!" Parris yelled, but she didn't get a response. "Where are you?" she asked. She walked into the room and noticed he was in the shower. She peeped inside the bathroom. "My friend is here, and I wanted her to meet you. But I guess she can later. I'm leaving. See you later. Bye," said Parris.

"OK. Enjoy your day," Brendan replied.

Parris closed the door and walked out to the living room. "He's in the shower right now. Are you ready to go?" Parris asked.

Not settling for Less

"Yes, I am. Let's get this girls' day started," said Janae.

"You know it, girl," Parris replied.

They got up and walked out of the house. As they were walking out, Brendan was getting out of the shower. He wrapped his towel around his waist and walked out of the room to see if Parris was still there, but as soon as he walked out of the room, the front door was closing behind them. Brendan glanced around the living room and noticed she was gone, so he went back into the bathroom so he could continue getting ready. He shaved his face, brushed his teeth, and brushed his hair after he was done with the basics; he put on his boxers and a white tank top and went into the bedroom.

Brendan's clothes were laid across the bed, so all he had to do was get dressed and head out. He put on his slacks, which he zipped and then buttoned. Then his dress shirt, which he buttoned up as well. He stepped in front of the mirror, looking as clean as a Bentley fresh off the lot. Brendan had a lot on his mind, but he was taking it one day at a time. He took a deep breath, grabbed his keys and his cell phone, and headed out through the door.

Chapter 13

Meanwhile, Parris and Janae had made it to Uptown Café before they got on their journey for the day—shopping journey, of course. In their eyes, there was nothing more exciting than some new clothes and shoes—every woman's addiction. They both had more shoes than they needed, but it seemed to never be enough. For every dress, there had to be a shoe to match. For every pair of shoes, there had to be accessories. This had become an addiction to so many, but it wasn't seen as one; it was just the life of a real woman.

A life where enough is never enough, where there is an endless assort of colorful jewelry. Hundreds of colors to match anything a woman could want or need when stores are closed. But now, they need to get ready to put the world off balance and have their man's eyes locked only on them like nothing else matters. A seduction tactic to make sure a man stays where he's at and doesn't stray like a mangy dog. Wearing something that he loves, also keeping it sexy and up to date. Men might seem like they are hard to keep, but just like you got him, you do the same to keep him—that's only if he wants to be kept.

Not settling for Less

Parris wanted to keep her man, but at that moment, she was trying to keep her mind off him, while Janae's mind was on the man that she thought was her man. There were secrets that could bring down a home as well as demolish any friendship—a friendship that Parris and Janae were growing fond of. They were finally seated and looked at the menu to see where their hunger would take them. Parris was looking at the steak tips, eggs, and grits, while Janae was looking at a southern omelet. They both had a big appetite this morning, and breakfast like the ones that caught their attention would definitely hit the spot. Parris licked her lips and said, "I know what I want; this steak looks great, and I've been wanting some eggs and grits for a couple of days now."

"I hear you, but I think I'm going to get an omelet. I haven't treated myself to a nice breakfast in a while, so why not today?" said Janae.

"I hear that," said Parris.

"I'm so excited; finally get to go out and hang out and, to top it off, go shopping," said Janae.

"I am too; I haven't been shopping in a while. Michelle is with her man most of the time, so I don't get a chance to

Chapter 13

hang with her much. I can understand that, though, but I still need to get out with the girls sometimes," said Parris.

"There is something I wanted to talk to you about," said Janae.

"Sure, we are having a girls' day out, so you can talk about whatever you want," Parris replied.

"I was thinking about letting my man out the doghouse; he seems like he learned his lesson. What do you think?" Janae asked.

"If you really think he has learned his lesson, then yes. Men are like babies at times. They whine; they get jealous; they need attention; and as soon as they don't receive any of it, they throw a fit. So, as a parent, you must discipline them to teach them that there are certain things that you're not going to put up with," Parris replied.

"I think he has learned. He has been looking pitiful lately. I think I'm going to show him some attention now, but enough about him. How are you and your man doing? I know last we were out, you said he did something and was in the doghouse. Did you ever tell him you were pregnant yet?" Janae asked.

Not settling for Less

"He's back in the doghouse. I'm hanging out now so I can get my mind off him. He had the nerve to stay out all night. He told me that he fell asleep in the car, but based on him messing up in the past, that's kind of hard to believe. I'm not stressing about it, though; just going to let him have the couch for a couple of nights until he wants to tell me the truth. He hates sleeping on that couch, certainly, for days at a time because his back and that couch don't get along at all," Parris said, laughing loudly.

"Yeah, that couch will break him right down, and you won't have to. That is too funny," Janae said with a laugh.

"Yes, that's momma's little secret to break his butt down. Anyway, this is our day, so let's enjoy ourselves," Parris said with a smile.

"I hear that," Janae replied as the waitress walked up.

"Hello, ladies! How are you doing today?" the waitress asked.

"I'm good," said Parris.

"Me too," said Janae.

"Great! So, what can I get you, ladies, to drink?" asked the waitress.

Janae and Parris looked at each other.

Chapter 13

"Well, I'll have some orange juice. Medium, please," said Parris.

"And I'll have a sweet tea. Thanks," said Janae.

"OK. Do you ladies know what you want, or do you still need a little time?" the waitress asked.

"We are ready," said both girls.

The waitress smiled. "OK," she said. She turned toward Parris and asked, "So, what can I get you?"

"Um ... I think I'm going to go with the steak tips," said Parris.

"White or wheat?" the waitress asked.

"Wheat," Parris replied.

"How would you like your eggs?" ask the waitress asked.

"Scrambled," Parris replied.

"Would you like hash browns or grits?" the waitress asked.

"I'll take grits," Parris replied.

"And how would you like your steak?" the waitress asked.

"Well done will be fine," Parris replied.

Not settling for Less

"OK, and for you?" the waitress asked.

"I'll take a southern omelet with white toast and grits. Thank you," said Janae.

"Great! Well, I'm going to put in your orders and bring your drinks. Was there anything else you ladies would like before I go do that?" the waitress asked.

"No, that's it," the girls replied.

The waitress left, and the girls talked and had a good ole time. About 15 minutes later, their food came, and they ate like they hadn't had breakfast in years. After they were done with their meal, they left and started their shopping spree.

Chapter 14

Chapter 14

The Second Encounter

Later that evening, the girls had finished their day off and were headed back to Parris's house. They had hit almost every store on that side of the sun and had bags loaded in the back seat like they had spent thousands of dollars, but they both had mastered the art of catching sales like they were certified shopping spree experts. The bags slid across Janae's leather seats like they had been greased down as her tires gripped the asphalt like a NASCAR corning the track. The smell of new clothes and shoes was like a natural high that had intoxicated the car. It smelled like the inside of a clothes store.

Meanwhile, while the girls were headed back to the house, Brendan was just about to head back also when he received an email on his phone; he pulled it up, and it was from his blackmailer:

Not Settling for Less

Hello, Brendan! I just wanted to thank you for handling everything in a manner to my liking. I know things have been a little frustrating for you, but I've been watching you for a while, and you're the kind of guy who sparks my interest, a guy who has everything, but for some reason, that doesn't seem to be enough. I never realized how many men like you existed until I met one of you for the first time, and I so much reviled his habits. I learned everything about your type, from the way you talk to the lies you tell, even the promises that never come to pass. Leaving women lost in a fantasy world where you only let them see and feel what you want them to, and nothing more. It almost sickens me that a man can have that much power over a woman's heart, and through it all, she remains blind to the truth. The truth that you will never leave your wife; the truth that you will never belong to just her; the truth that she will never get an honest word to come out of your mouth; that is something that I've grown out of because I refuse to settle. I refuse to become a victim of a game where you continue to win, and I continue to hurt.

I personally don't like how guys have the upper hand on certain things, so I decided to take matters into my own

Chapter 14

hands. I must take charge for all women to let them know they contain the power to let go and be free from the chains of manipulation that plague the world like racism slur tossed around like the "N" word, a word that our day and age can't seem to understand its meaning but continue to use as if it was a new addition to our language.

Just know these things that you guys are doing won't last, and you will all get what's coming to you. I'm only one woman, so my wrath is limited, but there will be other women who will get hipped to the game like I have, and they will handle it their way. I know you would like to know who I am, so I will give you that chance. I am addicted to sex, and I need to be taken care of one last time; then I will leave you be. I am no longer going to use the video against you; so, if you would like to get all your questions answered, meet me one last time and take care of me, and, in return, tomorrow, I will write to you and tell you my name and answer any question that you have.

It is 7:30 p.m. now, so come to Jefferson Park in an hour, and you will find a note on a bench marked with red

Not Settling for Less

spray paint. If you decide you don't want to come, then enjoy your life because it grows ever shorter day by day.

Brendan sat back in his seat in his car after reading the message. He wanted to be done with it and just leave it at that, but no matter how many times he shook his head, he still felt like he deserved to know who this woman was. She had so much control over his actions for a while, and she could have ruined his marriage at any time, but she didn't, so he wanted to know why. Why did she make him have sex with her against his will? He was angry and fascinated at the same time. He thought he always had the upper hand with everything, and when he didn't for that moment, it made him feel helpless, especially not being able to do anything about what she was doing. This was something that he didn't like at all; never in a million years would he have thought the tables would be turned around on him.

At this point, Brendan was thinking about his wife and that he was already on the couch, and if he went, most likely, he was going to be staying on the couch. So, he had to figure out if this was really worth it; the only thing he would be gaining is that he would know who this secret woman is, while he would be losing trust and damaging stability in his marriage. For some reason, he felt like this was a chance that he had to take so he could make sure this never happened to him again. Even though his wife would make him sleep on the couch until he started growing grey hair, he chose to meet her. So, he decided to text his wife to try and minimize the aftereffects.

"Honey, I will be home a little later. I didn't want you to worry. That's why I'm sending you a text," Brendan texted.

Meanwhile, Janae and Parris had made it back to his house, and they walked into the house.

"Baby, I'm back. Are you here?" Parris said in a high pitch. She walked into the room, looked around, and checked his office, but he was nowhere to be found. Suddenly, a text came through on her phone. She looked at the phone and walked back into the living room.

"He's not here. I wanted him to meet you. I guess he will have to meet you some other time," said Parris.

"It's OK," Janae replied.

"Bump him, though, because we had a blast today, and I can't wait until we can do it again," said Parris.

Not Settling for Less

"Girl, we can't do this much; you made me hurt my pockets a little today. I did have fun, though, but we might have to dismiss the shopping part," Janae said with a laugh.

"You're not bailing on me already, are you? I'm just playing. That's cool, though. We don't have to go shopping next time. We can go out to eat or something," Parris replied.

"Ya, because I don't own my own business yet, but I'll get there one day. We will do it again soon, though; just give me a couple of months to recuperate," said Janae.

"Really, girl, you're not that broke. Besides, I didn't make you spend anything that you didn't want to. All I did was take you to the places, so you could decide if you wanted it or not," said Parris.

"Ya, let you tell it. Anyway, enjoy your night. I have to call it a night, have to work in the morning. Goodnight, girl," Janae said as she hugged Parris.

"Goodnight, girl," said Parris as she walked Janae out.

Janae got into her car and started to drive off. Parris waved as she drove off; then she walked into the house, locking the door behind her.

Chapter 14

Brendan had made it to Jefferson Park, and it was 10 minutes before 8:30 p.m. He sat in his car, looking around the scene to see if by some chance he could see someone place a note on the bench. The sun was dropping down, and the light illuminated the leaves on the ground as the sky transformed from a light blue to a desert red, followed by all the colors that life holds, as the wind caused the trees to dance throughout the evening. The closer the sun got to the horizon, the fewer people he noticed. His eyes had to readjust as the light deemed down to a dark tone, which was soon to take over the park.

Brendan's eyes grew heavy as the darkness set in, and 8:30 p.m. hit like the last winning number of the fantasy five. His ticket to unlocking the mysteries behind all this madness was almost as clear as day. He took a step out of his car, a little nervous but anxious about what awaited him on that park bench. As he walked over, he couldn't help but watch his seat as he grew ever so closer to his destination. He finally made it to the bench; the park had become like a ghost town. The bench where Brendan had taken a seat was

Not Settling for Less

in a dark area where the lights couldn't reach, so it wasn't too visible and couldn't be seen by anyone passing by.

Brendan looked down to his left and noticed the note tacked down. He placed his finger over the tack so he could pull it up from the bench, only to find out that the tack was double-sided; it stuck him in the finger. "Ouch!" Brendan exclaimed, placing his finger in his mouth to stop the bleeding. He picked up the note and opened it; he couldn't see clearly, so he pulled out his cell phone to use the light from the screen to make out what the letter said:

I see you decided to come. I figured you wouldn't turn down finding out who I am. It's just something in you that wouldn't let you just let it go. Might call it a manly thing, but that's irrelevant at the moment. You're here, so, first, I would like you to know that the tack that pricked your finger has something on it that will weaken you quite a bit. I didn't want things getting out of hand, so I had to take precautions to ensure it didn't. So, when you finish the letter, it will have kicked in enough. You will be fully aware of everything; your touch, sight, and hearing will not be affected, but you won't be able to move.

Chapter 14

"What!" Brendan mumbled, as he could feel it kicking in.

It won't hurt you, and it will wear off in an hour or so. I wanted our last encounter to be exciting; you won't be able to move, but you will feel all the sensations and rush during the moment. I know you weren't expecting any of this, but that's one thing about life that's so remarkable; things seem to happen when you least expect them. Soon, you will have all your questions answered, and you will be on your way, and I will be on mine. We will be able to go our separate ways with no strings attached. I will have accomplished my goal, and you will be able to live your life—well, whatever number on life that God has given you based on your actions and how you live your life ...

"Whatever number God has given me?" Brendan said, looking confused.

... By the way, my name is Tami.

"Tami? Damn! Tami from the office," Brendan said, shocked by what he just read.

At that moment, his body grew weak, and he could hardly move. He placed his phone in his pocket and just sat

Not Settling for Less

there. A few seconds later, he noticed that he was being approached by a woman in a black trench coat. She walked near him in a seduction-paced walk, holding a stick-shaped object in her hand. She stood right in front of him, and he couldn't move a muscle. All he could do was watch as she slowly unstrapped the trench coat, and it started to slide off her shoulders down her curvy canvas of a body. Her luscious breasts sat in her silky trimmed bra, glistening as if they had been rubbed down with baby oil. A scent lingered through the air, twirling up the cavities of his nostril. The coat slowly slid over her hip, which was perfectly shaped; her caprice lit up his eyes like a dusty lamp.

Tami swayed her hips from the right to the left gently in an elegant manner. She was every man's fantasy; the body of a goddess cocooned in a silky vessel, that looked as if it would melt from a drop of water. Satisfying like Snickers that were just unwrapped. She leaned over and unbuckled his belt, unbuttoned his pants, and slowly zipped down his pants with her teeth as her breath grazed his lower abdomen. She reached into his boxers, braced his manhood firmly, and thrust it into her mouth.

Chapter 14

His knees felt like they wanted to buckle, but his body was unable to move, so the sensation continued to flow from his knees up his thighs and crept up his spine. Unable to move, all he could do was ease his eyes down so he could enjoy the sight of engulfment. She deep throated him like her tonsils needed a dancing partner, making his toes scream out because they couldn't curl up as needed. She came up for air, and her saliva dripped from her lips down his cock.

She pulled him forward, off the bench, and grabbed his pants on the right and left side; she slid them down to his knees and laid him back on the bench. Her fetish crop was dangling from her wrist, so she dropped her arm down so it could slide down enough for her to grip it; she rubbed it down the side of his face, down his arm, and to his thigh, rotating in a circular motion just enough to bring all the sensations to that precise spot; then she quickly popped him in that spot. He had never witnessed anything of that sort, but the feeling was remarkable.

Tami opened Brendan's eyes to a world that a lot wasn't too familiar with, for he wasn't as well. He looked at her as she pulled off her panties and spread her legs, placing

Not Settling for Less

her left heel on the bench beside his right arm, and her right heel on the bench beside his left arm. She eased down on him as she gripped the bench behind his head. "I want to feel you," she whispered in his ear, thrusting her pelvis against his with force as she sexed him like no other in a park that no one seemed to know existed during nightfall as the smacking of their skins paned through the trees. Up and down, she went like a cowgirl for 10 minutes.

She rode him fast and hard till she felt him burst inside of her, which triggered her orgasm, which made her legs grow tremendously weak. "Shit!" she screamed, leaning her head back as she gripped his neck tight. "Yes, that's what I'm talking about," she said as she slowly climbed down off him. "I can certainly say that you are blessed," she said, shaking her head as she got up. She put her panties back on and took a seat beside him. "Now that you know who I am, you won't see me again after tonight," she said, looking at him as she tried to plunder the thoughts that were flooding his mind. "I know you are wondering why and where I will be going. Just know it's just business, even though I enjoyed you. Why I did this? Well, that's a good question; so, listen up, and I will try to explain. I was taken advantage of; well, at

Chapter 14

least, my heart was. I was so in love with this guy, and he would always claim that he wanted to be with me and would make all these promises that never came to pass.

This went on for about three months, and then he just disappeared. He didn't call me, nor did he leave a note. He did leave something with me, though, and I've decided to pass on the heartache and unsoundness, for he had shown me that only blind individuals could be taken advantage of. Now that I'm no longer blind or weak to a smooth talker, I can now be the smooth talker and break a couple of hearts on the way and spread the legacy. Unfortunately, it's your turn; you have poisoned your marriage for years, and you were in control every step of the way, but it ends now. So, you can feel how it is to be fucked over for once." She got up, fastened her trench coat, and started to walk off. "Enjoy," she said as she walked off, swinging her crop.

Chapter 15

Chapter 15

Perplexed

Even though Tami had explained why she did what she did, Brendan still couldn't figure out why him. Why did she go through all that trouble to sex him the way she did and vanish in the gloominess of the night? Fifteen minutes had flown by, and the drugs had finally started to wear off. Finally, he was able to move his fingertips, then his arms. He turned his head slightly to the left, then to the right, as he stretched. She had left him with his pants down, and his cock lay on his thigh. That was his first time having sex out in public, and the rush was well worth it, but he didn't care about the aftereffects.

The first thing Brendan thought about was seeing Tami at work the following day, even though he wasn't quite sure if she was going to be there. She did say that he wouldn't see her again. *But how could someone just not show up to work?* he wondered. This had to be one of the most confusing days that he has ever had. A couple more minutes had gone by, and he was able to finally lean forward enough to pull up his pants. As he straightened up himself, he somewhat felt violated.

He had never been taken advantage of the way he had been tonight. He tried to stand to his feet, but his legs felt like he was trying to walk in a bounce house, so he collapsed back onto the bench. He felt like a baby who was taking his first steps again, and he couldn't help but grow frustrated. He was finally able to gather enough strength to stand to his feet and hold himself up on the bench. He scaled back and forth, up and down the bench like an old, crippled man. When he felt like he was able to make it to his car, he took a couple of steps at a time until he reached his car.

Unlocking his car, Brendan fell into the driver's seat and sat there for a minute until he felt like his reflexes were working well enough so that he could drive home. He knew his wife would question him, but it wouldn't be so bad because he wasn't out all night like he was the other night. He couldn't continue to sleep on the couch like he had been

Chapter 15

doing for the past few days. His back hurt just from thinking about it. This was something that he despised with passion.

He had finally gotten up enough strength, so he began to drive home before it got too late. He pulled out and drove like he had nowhere to be, and getting into an accident was something that he didn't need tonight. He just wanted to make it home safe and sound, with no issues. It was 10 p.m. when he pulled up to his house; he sat in the car for a moment so he could get himself together because Parris would be able to see a difference in his swag. Walking into the house slowly, it almost looked as if he had a few drinks; so, if that was the excuse he had to use, then he would run with it.

Parris walked out of the room and greeted Brendan. "Hey, you! Glad to see you made it home. Would you like to talk?" she asked as she stood there, waiting for an answer as she shook her left leg, not wanting to sleep alone tonight but was willing to do what she had to if he wasn't willing to step up and do what was right.

Brendan stood there, wanting to answer but not knowing how he would sound. Parris looked like she was being sincere, and he would rather spend another night on the couch than look stupid trying to talk. He didn't want to sound like he had a slur because then, she wouldn't want to talk to him at all. So, he just stood there.

"I guess not. Well, I'll leave you be. I guess we can try again tomorrow. Goodnight," Parris said. She turned and walked into the room, closing the door behind her.

The look on Brendan's face could only imitate how his body felt—pleased and depleted at the same time. All he could do was wobble to his place on the couch and try to get comfortable. He knew that soon; he would have to confess something to get past this jagged time in their marriage. He set his alarm on his phone, got his blanket, curled up on the couch, and dozed off.

The next morning, Brendan's alarm started to sound off. BEEP ... BEEP ... BEEP ... He reached over and grabbed his phone off the table; he looked at the time (7:30 a.m.) and then he hit the snooze bottom, wanting a few more minutes of sleep. Parris was running a little late and heard his alarm go off, even though she couldn't stand him at the moment, she still wanted to be a good wife, so she walked over to him, rubbed her hand across his chest, and whispered, "Time to

Chapter 15

get up, honey. Come on; let's get up. You need to get to work. I'm running late myself." She rubbed her hand across his head. "Get up, honey."

Brendan smiled gently and inhaled deeply as he tilted his body to the left slightly. He finally opened his eyes and looked up at Parris as she smiled, remembering the first time he saw her gorgeous smile light up his soul, stealing his heart forever. He remembered the times that they spent cuddling up on the couch, talking, as time faded away into eternity. She smiled as she walked down the aisle with a dress fit for someone no less than an angel.

She was in a frost-white gown that was created for her, and no other; he was her superman, and she was his damsel in distress. All the dirt, he did, and she stayed faithful through it all, keeping her covenant of love that she swore under the oath of God, dedicated to her husband through anything life brought their way. All these things made him love her, but the things he was doing to her were the same things that were killing him softly inside like a chronic disease, which was eating away at his soul.

Parris started to walk away. "See you later," she said.

Not Settling for Less

All the things that were in Brendan's head started to fade out the further Parris got away from him. His alarm went off again, and he finally swung his leg over the edge of the couch to the floor and whipped his hand over his face. Trying to wake up, those drugs somewhat had a sleeping pill effect. It wore off but had side effects that lingered over into the morning. He tilted his head back and then to the right in a circular motion, cracking his spinal bones. "Mmmm" he groaned.

Brendan leaned back on the couch for a moment, then rose to his feet and proceeded to the room so he could shower quickly and change into something a little more equipped for what his day held. Finally getting his mind right, he wanted to get to work to see if he could run into Tami before she split. He wanted to talk to her when he could respond back because being drugged up was not what he had in mind, and no matter how many times she spoke or explained something, it would never be enough until he could ask what he wanted.

Brendan finally pushed himself to get up and get moving. He walked into his closet, and his suits were lined

Chapter 15

down one side of the closet, while his everyday attire took vogue on the other. He had all kinds of suits lined up like a fashion parade—grey suits, brown suits, black suits, dark purple suits, navy blue suits, even white suits. Walking in his closet was like walking in the man's warehouse.

It was nicely placed, starting at the far end with an assortment of dress shirts, then slacks, and finally coats closest to the door. He had boxes of dress shoes: Rockport Men's Ellingwood, Cole Haan Williams, Marco Vittorio, Stacy Adams, and even Kenneth Coles. He had a basket of handkerchiefs, boxes of his collector-style watches, a closet of a bachelor—every man's paradise. He grabbed a frosty white dress shirt, with his Lauren taupe sharkskin classic suit. He grabbed some black dress socks, a pair of dark brown Marco Vittorio shoes, and his Calvin Klein Swiss brown leather strap watch.

This was a day that he would be sharper than a double-edged sword. Hopefully, he could step up to Tami, and she would know that he wasn't your everyday guy just in style alone, and maybe she would change the way she was handling him. He wanted answers, and he was trying to do what he could to get those answers. He laid his clothes

Not Settling for Less

across the bed, did a quick shave, and brushed his teeth. He was cheesing in the mirror as if he was auditioning for Colgate. After he checked his teeth, he gargled some mouthwash; then he went and grabbed some boxers and a tank top and then took a quick shower.

A few minutes later, he got out of the shower, dried off, put his boxers and tank top on, and then walked into the room, looking down at his exquisite suit. Putting his shirt on as it slid across his muscular arms, buttoning his shirt up to his Adam's apple. He put on his watch, then pinched his sleeve collar, pulling it down to his wrist, repeating the action on both sleeves. Sitting down at the foot of the bed, he slid on his socks, then his slacks. Standing to his feet, he tucked his shirt into his pants. Then he placed his shoes on the floor. He slid his feet into his shoes, tying them tight.

Walking over to his mirror and looking at his attire, Brendan turned his head to the side and noticed the time on the clock. "It's 8:20 a.m. Oh snap!" he said. He turned around and grabbed his coat, his suitcase, and his cell phone out of the office. He ran to the door, swiping his keys off the countertop by the door. He headed out through the

Chapter 15

door, locking the door behind him. He sprinted to the car. He jumped in and strapped his seatbelt across his chest. He cranked up his car and applied pressure on the brakes so he could put it into gear; then he pulled off. He let down the windows as he pulled off.

8:50 a.m. Brendan pulled up in the parking lot and hurried into the building. He walked into the office, dressed to impress. He was nervous but confident; he tied it all up in one. He looked around the office as he walked in, looking for Tami, but she was nowhere to be found. Janae noticed him dressed down and walked up to him. "Good morning, Brendan. How are you today?" she asked as she glanced at his suit attire. He was looking around, still on the search for Tami. Janae looked at him up and down like she wanted to jump on him right in the middle of the office.

Wanting to get rid of Janae so he could continue looking for Tami, Brendan replied, "Good morning. I'm good, and you?" He noticed that she was looking quite nice today, with a little cleavage showing, and a skirt that hugged her curves ever so gratefully.

Not Settling for Less

"I'm good," Janae replied, leaning over toward Brendan's ear. "I missed you and would like to see you soon," she whispered gently into his ear as she licked her luscious lips, rubbing her bottom lip across her lower teeth.

"Oh, really?" Brendan asked, looking at Janae, but his mind was elsewhere at that moment. So, he had to excuse himself from her so he could get some answers before it was too late, and he would be stuck in a state of confusion. "I'll be back. Please, excuse me for just a second," he insisted as he walked past her, trying not to make it too obvious that he was looking for Tami.

Brendan had enough problems as it is, and for Janae to think something was going on between him and Tami wouldn't pan out well. Janae was already upset about his wife, so another woman would be mayhem. So, Brendan walked as if he were walking to his boss's office for Tami's desk would be in sight. He made it to his boss's office and saw that he wasn't on a call, so he knocked, and his boss flagged him to come in. "How can I help you, son?" he asked as he looked at Brendan.

Chapter 15

Brendan turned around after looking at Tami's desk through the window and said, "Oh, I was just wondering where Tami was."

His boss looked at him. "She put in her two weeks' notice, and yesterday was her last day," he said as he wrote on some paperwork he had on his desk.

Brendan shook his head. "Wow, really? She just got here, though," he said, looking shocked as he whipped his hand across his face.

"Well, she said she didn't know how long she would be here. I let her work here because I was doing one of my friends a favor," Brendan's boss said. Brendan started thinking after being told this, as not only would he probably not see her again, but he also wouldn't ever be able to find out what this was really about.

"OK. She seemed like a good employee," said Brendan.

"Yes, she was actually pretty good at her job; it's a shame she had to go," Brendan's boss replied.

"OK, well, I'm going to get to work. Talk to you later, sir," said Brendan as he left the office.

Not Settling for Less

Walking back, Brendan was shortly joined by Janae as he entered his office, wanting to finish the conversation she initiated when he walked into the office earlier. Tailing him into his office, she shut the door behind her. Brendan turned and leaned back on his desk as she walked over and sat down in a chair beside him. Holding her head down, she said, "I missed you a lot, and I want us to get back on track. I was a little upset with you, but I think you have been on punishment long enough, and I would like to see you soon." She waited for his response, hoping that he felt the same. Even though he wasn't fully hers, Janae still loved the connection that they shared.

"Well, to be honest, I've missed you too, and you not talking to me didn't help rectify anything," Brendan replied. Her heart melted, but she had to hold herself together because she didn't want to show herself to be desperate or make him feel like she needed him, even though deep in her heart she did. Just the feeling of being wanted was enough for her at the moment.

"OK. Well, enjoy your day, and you look very handsome today, I must say. I'll talk to you a little later so we

Chapter 15

can set up something," Janae said as she got up and elegantly walked out of Brendan's office, her skirt showing him all the curves that she was blessed with. Brendan shook his head as he watched her walk out.

Chapter 16

Curiosity

Later that night, Brendan was in his office at home, working, when his wife walked into his office and looked at him as he worked at his office, not even aware that she was standing there in the doorway. She watched him as he wrote notes down on his notepad. He still had his dress clothes on from earlier and had his coat tossed across his desk. She looked at him like she wanted him right then and there, but she couldn't let him touch her yet, for there were still things that they hadn't talked about. No matter how sexy he was looking in that suit, she wouldn't become a victim of lust, at least not tonight.

She was going to talk to him, but she didn't want to disturb him at that moment, so she decided to wait until later. She started to move out of the doorway when his phone beeped. She usually wasn't the nosey type, but with everything going on, she decided to hide around the corner

Not Settling for Less

and peep so she could see his facial expressions. Brendan picked up his phone; he read the message and started to smile, and Parris started to boil inside because that wasn't a work smile; it was a lot deeper than that. She continued to watch as he completely stopped what he was doing, leaned back in his chair, and continued to message back and forth.

Every message he received, he had a smirk on his face, like finding out he was getting something he wanted for Christmas. She wanted to trust him, but all the crazy stuff that had been going on was really making that hard to do.

"So, when are we going to meet up?" Brendan received another text. He wasn't sure as he was already in trouble about the stuff that went down with Tami and was trying to figure out how to fix things with his wife at the moment.

"Not sure at the moment, but I will keep you posted," Brendan responded, not wanting to give her an exact time because he didn't know, anyway, at that moment.

Brendan continued to go back and forth for a few more minutes, unaware that his wife was lurking right outside his office door. She grew furious the longer she watched. Not wanting to snap at him, she decided to walk

Chapter 16

away; she didn't want to jump to conclusions too early. Even though she was quite sure he was texting another woman, she couldn't prove it, and she didn't want to accuse him and find out that she was wrong, so she let her curiosity build and decided to watch his every move until she had something tangible. Whenever she decided to bring things to his attention, she wanted to be ready for this lie he would probably fix his mouth to tell. It hurt her to think this way after all these years, but he was pushing her in that direction.

Brendan finally stopped texting a few minutes after his wife had eased away undetected. After putting down his phone, he glanced up to make sure he wasn't being watched. His actions were starting to make him feel paranoid, but it was too bad he didn't look up while his door was being patrolled. He was totally unaware of the hole that he was continuously making deeper. The things that he didn't notice would most likely be the ones that would condemn him. Focusing back on his work, he began to work again like nothing had happened; even though he was doing wrong and being scoped out, he didn't have an idea of what was awaiting him.

Not Settling for Less

About an hour had gone by, and Brendan was wrapping up the rest of his work and was about to shower and get ready for bed. He had a long day and just wanted some peace, no mystery messages, no work, no worries; he just wanted to relax. Placing his elbow on his desk, he leaned his head over, scratching his head softly and propping it up with his arm as he sat there for a minute, de-escalating because a million things were running through his mind. The more he tried to relax, the more his wife kept popping in his head; it was like a nightmare every time he even thought about doing wrong. It seemed like no matter how much he knew he was wrong, he always still ended up doing the same things over again.

Frustrated about what she had just seen, Parris didn't know what else to do than to try to get advice from one of her friends. She climbed into her bed, grabbed her phone, and texted Michelle, "Hey, girl; are you busy?" She waited a minute as she looked up at the ceiling. She grew impatient, so she sent one more text, "I guess you're busy or asleep, so I will hit you up tomorrow. Goodnight, boo." She still needed to get some things off her chest, so she was trying to see who she could text. Lying back in the bed, she said, "Oh, I know

Chapter 16

... Let me hit up Janae." She then texted, "Hey, Janae; do you have a few minutes?" She looked at the screen of her phone, waiting for a reply.

Finally, a couple of seconds later, Parris's phone lit up, and she noticed it was from Janae, and her face lit up in relief. She scrambled to respond. "Girl, I needed someone to talk to about my man, so I hope you can lend me your time for a little," she texted and waited for a response.

"Sure, you know I got you, girl. What's on your mind?" texted Janae.

"I was going to go talk to him, and I noticed that he was working, so I decided to wait until he was finished. Just when I was getting ready to walk away, he got a text, so I hid around the corner and watched to see what he would do. To remind you, he had already been acting funny and coming home at unreasonable times. But, anyway, when I was standing there, he was smiling and texting, so I know it wasn't his job. So, what do you think? Do you think he is messing with someone?" said Parris.

"Wow! Umm ... it sounds like he's up to something based on what you're telling me. You are better than me,

Not Settling for Less

though, because I would have confronted him right then and there. I don't really know any other reason he would be smiling like that," Janae replied.

"Ya, I'm pissed; that's why I needed someone to talk to before I responded and made things worse than they already are. I know myself, and I will go off if I don't calm myself," Parris texted.

"I know what you mean, but I'm here for you. Have you ever seen him do that any other time?" Janae asked.

"To be honest, I never really paid it much attention. I've always trusted him, so I wanted to give him his space and show him that I trusted him. So, if he was doing it, I never noticed it. I guess I was stupidly blinded by love. The way he's been acting lately makes me wonder if he has ever truly loved me," said Parris.

"I think he loves you; maybe it's not what you think. It's hard to say 100% what it is. Laughing could be from a family member or a homeboy as well. Just because he's smiling doesn't mean another woman is in the picture. Sometimes, we, women, are wrong because we let assumptions take over, and sometimes we place blame where it shouldn't be. I know because I've done it many

Chapter 16

times myself, and I can honestly say that's why I'm not in a relationship right now. I let what I thought form bad thoughts, and I acted wrongly, and this caused me to be by myself. Once you start thinking wrong, it usually takes over, and no matter how much a man isn't doing wrong, you still find fault in any and everything. The only thing that comes out of that is him getting fed up and leaving. You know we, women, don't like being wrong, but I was wrong, and it cost me my relationship. He wasn't perfect, but he did try to make things right, and at the end of the day, that's what truly matters. Now, I'm paying for it," Janae texted.

"I see you have been through a lot, and it's definitely not easy for us to admit we are wrong. You are surely right about that, lol. We like to be right about everything. Sometimes we know we are wrong and still will plead the fifth, lol. I am really trying not to start the assuming thing because I know it's hard to stop once you start it. We all make mistakes, and I'm sure God has someone lined up for you. Yes, you messed up with your ex, but everyone gets a second chance with love, and you have surely learned from your mistakes. When you're ready, he will come. It took me

Not Settling for Less

a while to find my husband, and I will be with him until we turn old as long, as he doesn't cheat on me, because I know my worth, and I'm worth way more than something like that," Parris replied.

"Yes, I'm sure we all have been through something at one point in our life. It all boils down to if we learn from it or not, and I have definitely learned, lol. I know I have things that I still need to work on, but that's surely not one of them, lol. I know He will send me someone; I'm hopeful it's my little boo that I've been talking to for a while now. That's a little complicated, though, and I'm not sure about that, but only time will tell. If he's not made for me, he will be removed from my life; if he is, he will stay put. We are talking about you at the moment, though. So, what are you planning on doing?" Janae texted.

"Not sure; I don't want to falsely accuse him, though, so I'm going to wait until I get more proof. I have to be careful because I don't want him to think I don't trust him. I'm getting close to not trusting him, though, but I'm going to make sure before I get to that point. It's just so frustrating at times; one thing I can say is, life is hard and gets harder by the day," Parris replied.

Chapter 16

"I know what you mean, girl. You will be OK, though, because I got your back. So, what are you going to do?" Janae texted.

"I appreciate that. Well, to be honest, I don't know yet. Oh, by the way, have you made up with your boo?" Parris replied.

"Well, I saw him at work, and I told him that I missed him and wanted to see him, and he said he missed me too. He also said we would schedule something sometime soon to hang out. I was thinking about a movie and dinner because we haven't been out doing anything in a while. We're usually just all over each other and don't really make it anywhere else, if you know what I mean. I guess that has a little to do with me, that we haven't been doing anything because I'm usually OK with us just chilling indoors. So, I need to change that before that's all we ever do, and one thing I don't want is for him to get tired of me," Janae texted.

"Oh, OK; that's good. I know what you mean, though. I need to get out and do more things with my man. Things get a little hard with our work schedules, though. When I get off, all I want to do is relax. Don't get me wrong; I cook dinner and

Not Settling for Less

make sure I take care of him when he's acting right. I always walk around the house with something sexy on. I keep the latest bra and panties, so I don't lose his attention; hopefully, it's working," Parris replied.

"I know what you mean because I try to keep up with my bra and panties also. Anyway, is your man still in the doghouse?" Janae texted.

"Yes, his butt is, and if he keeps going the way he is, his butt will stay in it. Yesterday, he came home, acting all funny; he kind of looked like he was drunk. I don't remember the last time he was drunk. I didn't say anything, though," Parris replied.

"Shoot! You are hardcore. I don't think I could make my man stay on the couch that long, knowing that it bothered his back. I would let him sleep in the bed, but he wouldn't be able to touch me," Janae texted.

"I suppose you're right about letting him sleep in the bed. I just want him to understand this isn't a game to me, and I'm not going to put up with his mess," Parris replied.

"I'm pretty sure he knows by now. How long has he been on the couch?" Janae texted.

"Going on a week now, lol," Parris replied.

Chapter 16

"Girl, you need to let that man get in the bed. Lol!" Janae texted.

"Lol ... I will," Parris replied.

"When? Next week? Lol ...," Janae texted.

"Anyway, so what's your man's name? You're always talking about him; so, what should I call this man of yours?" Parris texted.

"Oh, I never did tell you, his name. Well, his name is Brendan," Janae replied.

Parris stopped and read the text once more, thinking to herself. *Brendan? I know she isn't talking about my Brendan.* So, she decided not to say anything. She wanted to get a little more information to see if this really was him. A million and one things ran through her head at that moment—wondering if he was in his office texting her, wondering if she knew that Brendan was her husband. But before she jumped to conclusions, she had to get more information. "Oh, Brendan? That's nice. So how does this Brendan look?" Parris texted as she sat there, looking at her phone to light up with a response, hoping that Janae would respond with a different Brendan, but she was also anxious

Not Settling for Less

to know if this was the girl that he had been messing around with this whole time. Something of this magnitude would crush her heart; she had found a woman who seemed like a true friend, and even if she didn't know about her, it would be hard to keep her as a friend for the simple fact that she would think about them sleeping together every time she saw her face.

Just as all those thoughts were running through Parris's head, a message came through, "Well, he's about 5'11, light skin, with a great sense of style, and I can't forget he keeps a clean bald cut." As she read the message, her heart skipped a beat, but she still wanted to make sure it was him before she jumped to conclusions. A tear almost dropped from her eye; the only thing that stopped it from wetting her cheek was that she wasn't a hundred percent sure. But time would change that soon, as she sat back in her bed and started plotting a way to catch him in his tracks.

Not really in the mood to talk anymore, Parris replied, "Well, girl, I'm going to call it a night. Let me know when you're planning on going out to eat. Maybe I could see if my husband and I could join you guys. But don't say anything to your man because I'm not sure yet. Just keep me informed.

Chapter 16

Thanks for the talk; it really helped me make some sense of a lot," Parris texted with a devilish smirk on her face, ready to get the ball rolling. *"Let the game begin"*, Parris thought to herself as she curled up in her blanket while a spark of flame engulfed her eye in a darkened room, filled with hurt.

Chapter 17

Chapter 17

The Plan

That next day, Parris woke up and did what she usually does every day because she had to playthings cool until she had some hard evidence. She walked in and woke Brendan up from his sleep; she told him to get up before he was late for work. Once he was awake, she walked out of the house with a look of despise on her face. She was determined to get to the bottom of all these sneaky events that had been going on for some time now. This was probably the hardest thing she had set out to do; she had to skim up a plan of mastery expertise. Quiet but lethal was the only thing that was registered in her mind. A killer could get away with murder if his or her strategic planning was acrid. So, what she was trying to scheme up should be a walk in the park.

The more Parris thought about it, the more her stomach felt as if it would cramp up from the pain of a disloyal man. A man that not only promised her eternal love,

Not Settling for Less

but he also did it, looking God right in the face, and saying, "I do." She felt stupid for submitting to a husband who at the very moment seemed as if he was committing adultery. Maligning the word of God as she thought about how she had dedicated all these years of her life, what ate at the pits of her stomach the most was, that she was bearing a child who would be born into a world of twisted faith and sold lies. Every time she got the nerves to tell him of her pregnancy, his wrongdoings only darkened the conversation. Through all these dark clouds hid a truth that was smothered in the mystery dust of deception, one that was messing up this perfect world that she had lived in all these years.

Driving down the street, glancing out through the window, watching trees shuffle past her window like a whirled collage of your typical greens and browns which formed its arrangements, Parris noticed a couple prancing down the sidewalk, holding hands, swinging their arms like a swing set as they smiled and glanced into each other's eyes, reminding her of that spark that she and Brendan used to share. Outside, looking into a young woman's glow opens doors and edits illusions that she was blinded by from

Chapter 17

"love". The world captures a heart in the moment decaying the surrounding world as if it never existed.

Parris wondered if it was just a lust that overpowered and transformed her heart to only see what Brendan wanted her to see. Love may have been intertwined on her end, unsure of the darkness that lay in his. It's really a shame that she wasn't able to connect the dots from day one; perhaps connecting the dots wouldn't have let her win at the moment, or was it the expertise of her opponent to trap her in a love state?

Sometime later, Parris finally pulled up outside her job and got her mind right before she walked up to open the store and start her day. She got out of the car, walked up, unlocked the store, and walked in, locking the door behind her.

Meanwhile, Brendan was at work, being finessed by Janae. She was in his office, with the door closed, rubbing his shoulders. "How does that feel, baby?" she whispered in his ear, nibbling on his ear softly. Brendan leaned back in his chair, absorbing her gentle lips up against his ear, gazing up into her eyes as she pierced his shoulder muscles like she was certified in catering to his needs. She knew what to do and when to do it. He was so tense with everything that was going on at home, and that devilish couch wasn't helping either. He felt as if he was sleeping on a pavement slab every night.

So relaxed, all Brendan could do was mumble, "It feels great." Janae made him lean forward and slid her hands down his back, trickling her fingers across his back, and then applying pressure on his lower back and his upper back as she took her finger and swirled it around in a circular motion in the center of his back.

"I want to treat you out to dinner and maybe a movie. So, can you make some time for me tomorrow, please?" Janae said in a gentle voice as she continued to rub him down, keeping him equable, as he had his head almost plastered to his desk.

Brendan was so relaxed his mind had floated out of his office and into the atmosphere, where the only thing that existed was air and anything was free to fly, soaring the skies as the wind blew, feeling free like no handcuffs. He heard the question, but he wasn't thinking about the answer he was

Chapter 17

about to give. He was letting his high speak for him instead of thinking it through. "OK, why not? Just text me later and let me know what time and where, and I will make it happen," he replied. He was speaking because it felt right at the time, not aware of the situation that was going on at home. He was so lost in the moment; he didn't realize that it wasn't the best time to be going out, certainly not messing around.

"OK, baby. Thanks," Janae replied with a smile as she rubbed her hand across Brendan's back and down his right arm. She walked out of his office, rocking her hips slowly, for she knew he was looking. She opened the door and glanced back, puckering up her lips, blowing him a kiss.

Meanwhile, back at Parris's job, everyone had made it in. She had pulled Michelle into the office so she could talk to her about the situation. Still a little lost on how she should handle things, but she knew Michelle gave pretty good advice at times, and this time it was surely needed.

Michelle walked into the office, looking at Parris, as she looked as if she was going to burst into tears. She quickly rushed over to her, pulling her close in her arms. "Honey, what's wrong?" Michelle asked, removing the hair from her

Not Settling for Less

eye with her finger as she waited for Parris to mumble something.

Parris was trying to hold herself together, but as soon as she opened her mouth to say something, all the hurt and tears overpowered her emotions, and all she could do was cry.

"Parris, what's wrong, baby? Do you need me to fuck somebody up? Because you know I will," Michelle said as the look of someone pissed off conquered her facial expressions.

"I think Brendan is cheating, and you never will guess with whom," Parris said, shaking her head as she waited for Michelle to guess who.

"What ... Are you serious? With whom?" asked Michelle, looking shocked and wanting to avenge her girl at the same time.

Parris looked at Michelle and couldn't do anything but shake her head as tears streamed from her eyes.

"Who, girl?" Michelle asked again, wanting to know badly.

Chapter 17

"I'm not 100 percent sure, but I think Janae," Parris said as her heart trembled, body shivered, as she was unable to hold in the cry for help that her heart was letting out.

"What? Are you fucking kidding me? That bitch has been in your face all this time, and she has been messing with Brendan this whole time? I thought she was cool. Hanging with us, pretending that everything is cool. Smiling in our face when all along messing with your man! You know what? Just say the word, and I will fuck up her life, and I'm so serious," said Michelle. She paced around in the office and grabbed her purse. "Now, you know why I always keep something in my purse. Just say the word, boo," she said, looking at Parris right in the eyes, waiting for her to say something so she had permission to bring legal action.

"I don't know for sure yet. I was talking to her on the phone last night, and she mentioned his name because I asked her his name—well, her supposed-to-be man's name—and she said Brendan," Parris said as Michelle continuously paced around the office.

"Girl, I know you cursed her ass out. Please, tell me you cursed her ass out. If you didn't, I will curse her ass out!" Michelle was so amped up that all she could do was curse.

Not Settling for Less

"I don't believe this bitch! OMG! This bitch is so lucky!" Michelle blurted out several times.

"Michelle, calm down, please. I really need to talk to you about this. I need to come up with some kind of plan to catch him and her together. I really wanted to curse her out, but the more she talked, I could tell that she really had no idea that he's, my man. I think she doesn't know who I am. She might know that he has a wife, but I honestly don't think she knows it's me. So, I need to use that to my advantage. When we were talking, she was saying something about how she wanted to go out to eat and maybe a movie. While she was telling me all of this, I was trying to figure out how I could meet up with both at the same time while they are out," Parris said as she looked at Michelle, waiting for her input.

Michelle sat down, placing her elbow on Parris's desk as she rubbed her chin in deep thought. "First of all, are you sure she doesn't know?" Michelle asked.

"I'm sure. I even said that after, she let me know when, that I might be able to join her," Parris replied.

Chapter 17

"OK, good. You know what? I think I have an idea," Michelle said with a devilish look in her eye as she waited for Parris to get closer.

Parris scooted her chair closer. "OK, what do you think I should do?" she asked.

"OK. First, call her and find out the day and time. If they're going to hang out, she should know by now when and where. Once you get that information, we will go from there. If he is messing around, we are going to bust his ass like a pervert peeking through blinds," Michelle said with a smirk on her face.

"OK, I will, and we will go from there," said Parris.

"After you get that done ... then ..." Michelle told Parris what to do step by step. Parris grabbed a piece of paper and wrote down notes as Michelle continuously ran over everything. They talked for about 30 minutes, and when they were finished, Parris hugged her, and she exited Parris's office and went back to work.

Parris walked over to her desk, took a seat, and grabbed her phone as she leaned back in her chair. "Let the games begin," Parris said as she held her phone up, getting ready to text Janae.

Not Settling for Less

"Hey, Janae," Parris texted.

"Hey, how are you today?" Janae replied.

"I'm good. Just at work as usual," Parris texted.

"OK. So, are you and your husband good? Did you find out who he was texting?" Janae replied.

"Yes, I'm OK, and I think I have an idea who he was texting," Parris texted.

"OK. Well, hopefully, it wasn't bad as you were thinking," Janae replied.

"Still not sure about the whole thing, but I'm pretty sure it will all come to light in due time, so I'm not going to stress about it," Parris texted.

"That's good because you shouldn't stress. I'm pretty sure everything will be OK," Janae replied.

"Once I find out, I will surely let you know," Parris texted.

"OK. So, how's your day going so far?" Janae replied.

"It's going OK so far. The store is busy as usual, and I also got a chance to talk to Michelle, and she eased my mind a little as well," Parris texted.

Chapter 17

"OK. Work is a little busy over here as well. I can't wait to get off," Janae replied.

"Oh, by the way, did you ever find out when you were going to be hanging out with your man yet?" Parris texted.

"As a matter of fact, I did. Well, somewhat. I asked him today, and he said to text him with the date and time, and he would make it happen. I was thinking about tomorrow evening," Janae replied.

"Oh, OK. So, where are you planning on going for dinner?" Parris texted.

"Jimmy's Seafood, off Clark Road, around 6 p.m. Then, after that, hit movies about 8 p.m. at the theater down the street on Hicks Ave.," Janae replied.

"I see you have it planned all out," Parris texted.

"Yes, I do. So, were you planning on joining us?" Janae replied.

"I was thinking about it. I don't know if I can make dinner, but the movie might work better," Parris texted.

"OK. Well, if not, it's cool. We can always do it another time," Janae replied.

"You're right, but I will keep you informed," Parris texted.

Not Settling for Less

"OK, great," Janae replied.

"Well, I will text you tomorrow at about 7 p.m. to let you know about the movie, and do me a favor; can you not tell your man? I'm not going to tell my husband either. I want it to be a surprise if that's OK with you," Parris texted as she grinned, with a sneaky look on her face, because she knew she had Janae right where she wanted her, and she had no clue what was going on. She was so ready to catch Brendan in action and watch him as he stood there with his mouth wide open. Getting caught was the last thing he expected. So many years that he has been sneaking around, while she trusted him. It hurts, but she needs to see it for herself. *Just crazy how all this is happening before he even found out that he has a baby on the way*, Parris thought.

"OK, that's not a problem; we can keep it a surprise," Janae replied.

"Well, I will talk to you tomorrow; enjoy the rest of your day," Parris texted.

Chapter 18

Chapter 18

Suspicion

The next morning, Parris woke up and did her everyday routine. She woke Brendan up as if nothing was wrong, with a look on her face as if nothing was running through her head, when all along she wanted to chop off his manhood and feed it to the Sharks. She usually felt bad about him sleeping on the couch, but today, there was nothing, no feeling of remorse whatsoever. After she had made sure he was up, she headed out. She didn't want anything messing up the plans for the day, so his schedule had to go accordingly.

Parris jumped into her car and headed to work, while all her thoughts tossed and turned in her head like a bad night of sleep. She and Michelle had come up with a plan that couldn't fail unless Janae herself changed them. Parris had something set up so she could find out everything that was going down from the time Brendan got off work.

Not Settling for Less

Meanwhile, Brendan had gotten up and started to get ready for work when a text came through from Janae: "Tonight, at 6 p.m., meet me at Jimmy's Seafood."

"I see you didn't waste any time setting up something," Brendan replied.

"I asked, and you said, 'Let me know the when and where,' and you would make it happen. So, I'll see you later, right?" Janae texted.

"You're right. I will be there. You know Jimmy's Seafood is one of my favorite places to eat, anyway. You knew exactly what you were doing," Brendan replied.

"Well, I wanted to treat you to somewhere you liked," Janae texted.

"Wow, you are treating too," Brendan replied.

"Yes, I am. I can treat my boo sometimes," Janae texted.

"OK, sounds good. Well, I'll see you at work," Brendan replied.

"OK," Janae texted.

Brendan looked at the last message, placed his phone on the bed, and continued to prepare himself to leave.

Chapter 18

Not wanting to get questioned later, he decided to get out something casual to wear later and just leave it in the car; that way, when he left, things didn't have to seem more obvious than they already were. He had a small handbag, so he threw some slacks in, a purple V-neck dress sweater, and some purple chucks.

It wasn't too much and was comfortable to wear out as well. After getting his clothes together, he jumped in the shower to get freshened up before heading to work. His back was aching, so he turned the hot water up full blast and stood under it as the water slid down his back, soothing his aching muscles. After receiving a little relief, he finally got out of the shower and got dressed.

Later that day, Brendan was at work when a text came through. "Good afternoon. I just wanted to let you know that I was going out tonight with Michelle for a little," Parris texted.

This was perfect because he didn't have to worry about trying to explain where he was headed later. Little did he know it was not in his best interest how things were playing out. It sounded good at that moment, but only time would reveal its true purpose. "OK," Brendan replied.

Not Settling for Less

The day had flown by; Brendan was off and was headed to meet up with Janae at Jimmy's Seafood, but first, he had to run to the car and grab his bag out of the car to change before he left. He got dressed and was more comfortable. He loved suits, but it felt good to take off his work clothes.

He placed his clothes in his bag, sprayed on some cologne, and exited the building. This was the first time he wasn't uncomfortable about going out with Janae; maybe because he knew most likely Parris would be at Michelle's house, and she wouldn't be worried about what he was doing. So, the smile on his face was a little more than usual; he was ready for a night of relief from everything that had arisen and had his marriage on the rocks.

Brendan finally pulled out of the parking lot and started heading towards Jimmy's. He wanted to show Janae how much he missed her now that he didn't have Tami taking up his time anymore and having him looking like a lost cause. He wanted to do a little something extra, so he stopped by a gas station and grabbed a single rose, not realizing that he would be in trouble if he got caught slipping, even though

Chapter 18

that was the last thing that took a voyage in his mind. A hard shell to crack, but if and when it does, it will shatter all over his life. Something that he wouldn't bet on, but when you play with the devil, sooner or later, things will get hot.

Brendan pulled up to the gas station at about 5:30 p.m., about 15 minutes from his destination. He rolled up his sleeves as he stepped out of the car to purchase a red beauty for his black beauty. Luckily, there was a single rose left. Looking down at the price as he picked up the rose, he said, "$4.50? Dang! The gas station is getting over on people." He shook his head as he handed it to the clerk, hoping the price was wrong.

The clerk rang up the rose. "That will be $4.77," said the clerk.

Brendan paid for the rose, snatched it off the counter in disappointment, and rushed out of the store to head to his favorite restaurant, where he would be spoiled for the evening.

Meanwhile, Janae had made it to the restaurant at 5:50 p.m., where she had made reservations for the evening. Her phone beeped from a text message, and she grabbed it out of her purse to respond. She replied to the text and then

Not Settling for Less

placed her phone back inside her purse as she looked at the door, she heard a squeaky sound from the door opening as a couple entered; she was checking to see if it was Brendan.

About 10 minutes later, Brendan walked in the door, and Janae looked at him like she wanted to have him for dessert after the main course meal. Her eyes scaled up his light brown slacks, then across his purple sweater, and locked in on his seducing smile.

She rose to her feet as he walked towards her, with one hand placed behind his back. Once he was standing right in front of her, he pulled his hand from behind his back and said, "Here is a gorgeous rose for a stunning woman. You look absolutely breathtaking in that white dress. Damn, girl! We might have to skip dinner and head right to dessert." He looked at her up and down as he held her hand and stepped back, twirling her around in a circle so he could see every curve.

"You're a trip," Janae said with a smile.

"Girl, I'm on vacation, but let me get my mind out of the gutter. Shall we?" Brendan asked as he guided Janae toward the host booth so they could be seated. He hadn't

Chapter 18

eaten all day and was ready to get his favorite so he could go to town.

"Hello! So, Janae, are ready to be seated?" the host greeted them.

"Yes," Janae replied with a nod.

The host grabbed some menus. "OK, this way," she said, leading them to their table, which was decorated with black-laced tablemats, and white-and-black cloth napkins that wrapped the silverware. They took a seat. The décor lamps hung overhead created just enough light for their dining pleasure.

"Your server will be with you in just a second," said the host as she placed the menus in front of each of them.

"Thank you," they both replied.

"So, I would ask you how your day was, but seeing that we work in the same building, I have a pretty good idea how it was," said Brendan.

"You're so crazy. I'm just happy to be off. I missed you, and I've been anxious all day, waiting for this moment," said Janae.

Not Settling for Less

"Ya, I've been a little anxious myself, and seeing that you picked my favorite restaurant didn't help at all," Brendan replied.

"Yes, I knew it was your favorite restaurant, but what's a girl to do when she wants to spend some time with her boo? We have been a little distant from each other lately. I can admit I was a little mad at you, but that didn't last too long, as you can see. A week was long enough for me," said Janae.

"Oh, really? You were mad at me?" Brendan asked.

"Yes, but it's over now; let's just enjoy dinner so we can get out of here and catch our movie later," said Janae.

"OK. So, let's see what I'm in the mood for tonight. Choices ... choices ... choices ...," said Brendan.

They both chose something and placed their order; they talked until the food came. Once the food came, they ate and enjoyed each other's company. About 7 p.m., Janae received another text; she responded and put her phone back up.

At about 7:30, she and Brendan had just finished eating; they took care of the bill, tipped the waitress, and

Chapter 18

headed out so they wouldn't be late for the movie. They walked out, got into their cars, and tailgated each other to the movie theater. About 15 minutes later, they pulled up to the theater and parked beside each other.

Meanwhile, Parris and Michelle waited for Janae and Brendan to walk into the theater.

Parked in the front, with so many people there, it would be pretty hard to spot them. Janae and Brendan got out of their cars and hugged each other; Brendan grabbed her butt. Then they held hands and started walking through the parking lot, towards the building.

"Girl, I don't see them. Are you sure this is the theater she was talking about?" Michelle asked as she looked at everyone who had walked by; she didn't notice Brendan or Janae anywhere.

"I'm pretty sure this is the one. Let me check my messages again," said Parris as she and Michelle glanced down at her phone. At that moment, while they had their heads down, Brendan and Janae walked by, holding hands. It's almost like time slowed down for just a second as Parris and Michelle were going back and forth about the theater. Brendan and Janae couldn't have walked by at a more

Not Settling for Less

perfect time. As soon as they walked into the building, Michelle glanced up and missed them by a few seconds.

"See, this is the right one. She said the movie started at 8 p.m.," Parris said, holding up her phone so Michelle could see it.

"OK. Well, I guess we need to keep looking, then. I can't believe she was the one that Brendan has been messing with this whole time," Michelle replied.

While they were talking in the car, Janae ran into her cousin while she was in line, getting popcorn. "Janae is that you?" her cousin asked.

Janae looked around. "Hey, James! What are you doing here?" she asked.

"I was just trying to get out of the house. Oh, you know I left my charger in your car," said James.

"OK. Well, after the movie, I will get it for you," said Janae.

"OK, cool. See you then," said James.

Janae and Brendan got their popcorn and drinks and headed into the movie. Afterwards, Brendan and Janae came out of the movies; and James was waiting so he could get his

Chapter 18

charger out of Janae's car. Brendan had to take a leak, so he told Janae that he was going to the bathroom, but before he went in, she said, "Meet me at the car; I'm going to walk out with James so I can give him his charger."

"Ok, I'll see you at the car," Brendan replied with a nod as Janae walked off.

Parris and Michelle ended up waiting in the car until the movie was over. Michelle was wide awake, but Parris had dozed off. Finally, after an hour and a half, she noticed Janae coming out of the theater, but to her surprise, Brendan wasn't walking beside her as she exited the building.

Michelle reached over and tapped Parris, and as she opened her eyes, Michelle was pointing at Janae walking by. Parris felt so bad that she was out, trying to catch her husband, and it wasn't even him.

"I think I'm going to head home now. I feel so stupid to even think that Brendan and Janae were messing around," said Parris. She shook her head and started up the car.

"It's OK. There was no way for you to know, but now you know; so, you can ease your mind," Michelle replied as she looked at Parris, who looked miserable.

Not Settling for Less

"I can't believe I'm out here, doing this. I should just trust my husband instead of being out here, trying to spy on him. I guess I'm the fool," said Parris. She put the car in drive and rode off. "I'll take you back to your car," she said to Michelle.

A couple of seconds later, Brendan walked out, but Parris was too far away to notice him; her backlight illuminated the darkness like it was painted in red. He walked over to Janae's car; she was saying goodbyes to her cousin. Brendan walked up to her, "Would you like to walk through the park before we head our separate ways?" Brendan asked.

"Sure! That sounds nice; I wasn't ready to leave you, anyway," said Janae. They both jumped in their cars and headed down the street to the park.

Parris had just made it to Michelle's car. "Thanks for coming with me, girl; you're always there for me," Parris said; she reached over and gave Michelle a hug.

"Of course! You're my best friend. Well, get home safe. I'll see you tomorrow at work," said Michelle.

Chapter 18

Parris headed home and felt horrible about what she had done. The more she thought about it, the worse she felt, so she turned on her music and maxed out the volume, despite how she felt, to calm her mind.

Chapter 19

Intuition

It was 8:50 p.m., and Parris had made it home. Then she went to see if Brendan was home, but he wasn't, so she sat on the couch, but no matter how much she accused herself of being wrong, there was something deep inside her that forced her soul to turn like something wasn't right. She played back the conversation that she and Janae had over and over in her head, but something didn't seem to add up. The guy that was with Janae was clean-cut, but he didn't have a bald head. She picked up her phone and checked the message to make sure it wasn't just her emotional state that was causing her to think this way. After scrolling through her messages, she found that she was right.

Well, the text was right; could it be possible that Janae had texted the wrong thing? For words don't lie; only the people who tell them. Parris also was a little drowsy, but the guy who was accompanying Janae had a darker skin

Not Settling for Less

complexion than Janae had expressed before. Parris just wanted to drop it, but she just couldn't let it go. She decided to make sure her mind wasn't playing tricks on her. She picked up her phone and wanted to text Janae and ask where she was. She fought the urge to for a couple of minutes; then she just couldn't help it.

"Hey, Janae! How was your date? Sorry, I couldn't make it," Parris texted.

Janae and Brendan had just made it to the park and were walking when a text came through, so Janae stopped to check her phone. "Hold up, baby," Janae said as she checked her phone; she noticed it was Parris. "It was good. Thanks for asking. We went to dinner, then to the movies, and now we are walking in the park. I hope your day wasn't too stressful," Janae replied.

"Girl, you have no idea. I need a drink," Parris texted.

"I hear you on that. I get that way too," Janae replied.

"You said you guys were at the park? What Park did you guys go to?" Parris texted.

"Oh, we are at Samson Park, but I'll give you all the info tomorrow. I don't want to be rude☺," Janae replied.

Chapter 19

"OK, girl. Enjoy," Parris texted. She got on her phone and googled Samson Park, and it was about 15 minutes away, so she jumped up, grabbed her keys, and headed over there.

While Parris was driving, she texted Brendan, but she got no response from him. He usually responds, so, in her mind, he had to be doing something. The closer she had got; it seemed like she was catching every light on the way over there. 15 minutes later, she arrived at the park, and she noticed Brendan's car parked, and immediately, her anxiety peaked. "I knew it," she mumbled as she parked at a distance so she could peep out the scene. "So, he was messing with her? I can't believe this shit!" Parris said in a pissed voice, looking around at anything that moved. "After all we have been through, he is out here, messing around on me!" Parris said as she sat in her car, waiting to see Brendan with Janae.

About 20 minutes had gone by, and Parris finally saw Janae, but it was fairly dark, so she couldn't really see if the guy she was walking with was Brendan or not, so she started up her car and slowly rolled closer to them, with her lights

Not Settling for Less

off. "Man, I swear this better not be Brendan's ass," she said. She had finally gotten close enough to see.

Brendan noticed a car creeping as he turned around. Right then and there, Parris's heart was crushed to see him standing there, looking like he didn't realize that he was married. Not that he even cared, for the most part, but just the sight made her heart feel as if it would burst.

Before Parris knew it, she pulled the car right over to the curb and jumped out, and the look on Brendan's face said a million words while he stood there, unable to mutter one word. Janae still didn't have a clue who Parris was to Brendan.

"Hey, Parris! What are you doing out here, girl?" said Janae.

"Janae, I know you have no clue on what's going on, so just be quiet for a second, please," said Parris.

"Huh! What do you mean?" Janae asked as she looked up at Brendan, who was looking like he had just seen a ghost.

"Ya, Brendan, why don't you tell her what's going on?" Parris said, looking at Brendan like she wanted to fight him right then and there.

Chapter 19

"That's what I thought; you don't have anything to say. So, Janae is who you have been messing with this whole time, huh? I so can't believe you right now. You have the nerve to be out in public with another woman when you know you're married. I gave you my life, Brendan, and this is what you have the nerves to do," said Parris, holding up one finger and pointing it as tears started streaming down her face. "I so can't deal right now. If you knew how I feel right now," she said, shaking her head. "I gave you my fucking heart, Brendan, and this is how you repay me. You're supposed to be my fucking husband," Parris said as she started pulling her ring off her finger. As bad as she wanted to throw it at him, she didn't; she just handed it to him and turned to Janae. "I feel sorry for you to have to deal with a man like this. I know you had no idea I was his wife, but I do know you had an idea that he was married, so you deserve just what you have coming to you. He messed around on his own wife, so what makes you think for one second that he wouldn't do the same to you? But it's cool because you guys deserve each other. I have no hard feelings for you; I'm just hurt right now. I know you're a good woman, but you're going at getting a

Not Settling for Less

man the wrong way. When you interfere with what God has done, no good will come of it. I will pray for you, though," Parris said, shaking her head at Janae.

"Baby, I ...," Brendan mumbled, but before he could get out a word, Parris interrupted.

"You are nothing but an impostor. Oh, and by the way, I am pregnant with your baby. I was waiting for a good time to talk to you, so what better time than now. Don't worry, though; I won't put you on child support, and neither do I care if you want to be in our child's life. All I want from you at this moment is for you to come get your stuff and leave. We will be fine all on our own," said Parris.

"You have been pregnant all this time and haven't told me, "Said Brendan.

"Oh, do you mean like you haven't told me that you have been messing around all this time? Interesting. You stand here and want an explanation about me not telling you something, but you haven't said one word about why you're out here, screwing around. I know my worth, and I know it's more than what you're trying to offer. Just come get your stuff out of my house, please," Parris replied.

Chapter 19

"So, you're just going to put me out? We can't talk about this?" Brendan asked.

Janae looked at Brendan with disgust. "I'm sorry, Parris. I didn't try to hurt you. I had no idea it was you Brendan kept telling me he would leave for me. He never told me your name, how you looked, or anything. But I am truly sorry for everything," Janae said as she handed Brendan back the rose, he had given her and walked off.

Parris turned around, walked over, jumped back in her car, and drove off. On her way to the house, she called the police. "There is a man at my house, and he won't leave. I live at 2200 North Cryer Street," Parris said then she hung up the phone. Making it back home, she waited for Brendan to pull up as she stood in the front room, trying to hold in all her emotions. Brendan pulled up a few minutes after her and walked into the house.

Walking in, Brendan stood there for a second. "Baby, can we please talk about this?" Brendan asked.

"Talk about what?" Parris replied.

"Us and our marriage," said Brendan.

Not Settling for Less

"Do you mean the same one you have been committing adultery in?" Parris asked.

"I want to be here for you and the baby," said Brendan.

"Really, Brendan? Before you knew it was a baby, you weren't trying to be here. You have been out there, screwing around on your wife. Just get your stuff and leave. Get what you need for tonight, and we will set up a way for you to get the rest of your things," said Parris.

"This is my house too; I'm not getting out," said Brendan as he noticed police lights through the window. "Did you call the police?" Brendan asked as he looked out of the window.

KNOCK! KNOCK!

Brendan opened the door. Looking at the officers standing in the doorway, he asked, "Can I help you, officer?"

"Yes, we received a call. Is there anyone else here with you?" asked the officer.

"Yes, officer. I called you guys. I would like him to leave my house," said Parris.

"What did you call the police for?" Brendan asked in an angry voice. Parris stepped back.

Chapter 19

"Sir, can you please step out of the house?" the officer asked.

"What do you mean? This is my house too," said Brendan.

"Sir, can you step out of the house, please?" the officer asked once more.

"Officer, this is my house too," Brendan replied.

"Is your name on the lease," the officer asked.

"I think so," Brendan replied.

"OK. Well, step out of the house, and we will find out what's going on, and we will go from there, but I need you to work with me and step out of the house, sir," said the officer.

"OK," Brendan said as he looked back at Parris, shaking his head. He walked outside and stood by the other officer in the police car. He watched while the other officer was at the door, talking to his wife. He was so mad that she would call the police; his face expressed every feeling that he held inside. He was so shocked that he even got caught; he felt stupid and bad for hurting his wife, even though while he was doing it, he couldn't have cared less about how she felt.

Not Settling for Less

It must have been because he hadn't been caught yet, so he paid no mind. Now that everything has happened, he actually feels bad about it. He knew he was wrong for sleeping around then, but to see Parris cry really got to him. He knew there was probably nothing he could say to make her take him back, but besides that, he couldn't even think of anything to say. Saying sorry wouldn't even help because it didn't bring him home on the nights he should have been there. While all those thoughts passed through his head like rushing traffic, the officer who was speaking to his wife came out and walked to the car.

"So, can I go back into my house, officer?" Brendan asked.

"Sorry, I can't let you do that. I spoke to your wife, and she wants you out. Your name isn't on the lease, so, technically, she doesn't have to let you in to get anything out of the house, but she is being nice. She said you can go pack some things you will need. I will walk you in and let you get what you need; then I will walk you back out," said the officer.

"Wow, are you serious? All my stuff is in there," said Brendan.

Chapter 19

"I hear you, sir, but that's a matter you will have to take up with the courts unless she will work on some kind of agreement where you can get your things, which I'm sure she will; she just wants you out tonight, and you guys can settle your differences on another day. So, let's just take care of this tonight and worry about everything else tomorrow," said the officer.

"OK, well I'll grab a couple of things and leave," said Brendan.

"OK. Well, come on, and I'll wait outside the room until you get what you need," said the officer as he followed Brendan into the house to grab his things.

Brendan walked in and saw Parris sitting on the couch, with her head down, unable to look at him. She was so hurt and disgusted by him that she didn't want to waste her view on someone so low. She had put up with a lot from Brendan, and this was the last straw. A couple of minutes later, Brendan walked out of the room with his bag and stopped. "I know this will probably not mean anything, but I'm sorry, and I hope you forgive me for hurting you," Brendan said; then he turned and walked out the door.

Not Settling for Less

Parris looked up as Brendan turned around. "I do forgive you; just will never forget. Bye."

Chapter 20

The Shocking Truth

Brendan was so depressed; not only had he lost his wife, but also, he also wished that he had done right so he could live a life with a family that he knew he would have loved. He couldn't blame anybody but himself, and worse, Janae wouldn't talk to him, no matter how many times he called; the ringer had started to grow numb. The ringer echoed from the phone to the dry walls in the hotel room that he was occupying for the moment. If he didn't realize what being lonely was, it was surely paying him a visit now. He had never felt anything like this before, and it was killing him. All that kept running through his head was how his wife was looking when she caught him walking in the park with Janae.

The room had become a depressing layer of darkness that floated over his head like a dark cloud raining nothing but bad memories that he had created and now had to live with. What ate him up the most was that he wouldn't be able

Not Settling for Less

to be in the household with his son, for that was something that he missed as a child, and he always used to say that he didn't want the same thing to happen when he had a child. The one thing that he didn't want to happen in his family trickled right down into his life like the waterfall that had flooded his childhood and a father that he never got a chance to witness.

Leaving him without a chance to see what it felt like. How it felt to play catch with his father or go sit out on the lake and catch a bucket full of fish. This was something that he had to bear when he was younger. Having a deadbeat dad, who walked out on him and his mother like a CIA agent who had gone deep undercover, was tragic. After a while, his mind went numb also, and all he could do was stare at the wall that was his only company as he listened to the news talk about all the tragic things that were going on in the world.

He heard about people who had fallen to another bullet from another deranged law enforcement officer; how riots were starting because of the under-ruling of sentenced time; judges were pretty much giving out, get-out-of-jail-free cards like meal tickets. He also heard about hit-and-runs and all the violence between his fellow men. It seemed like

Chapter 20

the world was full of disorder, and the more and more news he heard didn't make him feel any better.

Suddenly, Brendan's phone rang, and without looking at the number, he answered, "Hello."

"Hello, Brendan. How are you?" said Parris.

He sat up straight. "Hey, I'm hanging in there, and yourself?" said Brendan.

"I'm good; I know you're surprised I'm calling you. To be honest, I am, too. Never thought you would ever hurt me the way you did. It took me a little time to get over it, and I forgive you. I know how things were when you were a child, and I'm not trying to have our son go through the same thing. So, I would like for you to be in your child's life. The last thing I want to do is make you feel like I'm taking your son away from you because I'm not. Just because we can't work doesn't mean you and your son can't have that bond that you never had with your father. I should be having him within the next month; so, if you want to be in his life, I will text you when it's time," said Parris.

"I would like that; thank you," Brendan said as a tear dropped from his eye.

Not Settling for Less

"Well, take care of yourself. You messed up, but it's not the end of the world, so keep your head up. Talk to you later," said Parris.

"OK, bye," Brendan replied.

"Bye," Parris responded.

As soon as Brendan got off the phone, he saw Tami on the news. She was being arrested. He zoomed in and turned up the volume.

"Young black woman was being arrested today for first-degree murder," said the newscaster.

"What?" said Brendan.

"This young lady was going around, sleeping with men, infecting them with HIV. She was going to Westfield Resort and had become a regular to the employees. The resort manager felt something wasn't right, but she couldn't deny a room to a paying customer. She said she had been checking in at least once a week for the last five months. She would put the room in the guy's name and let them check in and was given an extra key when she arrived," said the newscaster.

"Are you fucking kidding me?" said Brendan.

Flashback:

Chapter 20

I've decided to pass on the heartache and unsoundness ... Your actions and the way you live life pulled me towards you ... Unfortunately, it's your turn; you have poisoned your marriage for years, and you were in control every step of the way, but it ends now ... So, you can feel how it is to be fucked over for once ...

Everything hit Brendan like a ton of bricks; Tami was setting him up the whole time. He was so at a loss for words that all he could do was pass out.

Somewhere in a penthouse, an 80-inch TV was sitting on a glass stand, in front of glass windows that were lacing the entire room from the floor to the ceiling. The view was dark, but one could still seem to catch the waves crashing the shoreline.

A woman sat in a plush white chair, her legs crossed and clad in white fishnet pantyhose, paired with red stilettos. As she watched the news, her leg bounced up and down with agitation, her eyes fixed on the scene of Tami being led away in handcuffs and placed in the back of a police car. Suddenly, she clenched her fist and slammed it onto the table beside her, her voice rising in an anguished cry:

Not Settling for Less

"Noooooooo....!" The sound echoed through the empty house like a desolate stadium, her eyes blazing with fury as they pierced the TV screen. Her teeth gritted together in rage, her anger and frustration palpable.

To Be Continued

Word of Wisdom

Words of Wisdom

Some of the hardest things in life are set before us, but it's our choice whether we settle for them or not. Your happiness is everything, so appreciate it. Take control of your life; enjoy your life while you can. It's never too late to start over. There is someone for everyone, so open your eyes and let go of the things in life you don't truly want or need. There is always a way out; you just need to find the door, and your determination to want better will be the key that will unlock that door to a better life. There is so much more to life than heartache, deception, and manipulation. Your life is just that—your life. So, treat it as that and be happy with someone who makes you happy. Believe in yourself, know your worth, and leave the foolery right where it is. You deserve better in life, and the only way to get what you deserve in life is by *Not Settling for Less*.